# LESEDI

## and the

# PURPLE LOTUS

# LAUREN BROOKS

Winn Publications, FL

ISBN: 979-8-9871422-3-3

Winn Publications LLC, Florida

winnpublications.com

# LESEDI

## and the

# PURPLE LOTUS

Dedicated to my sons.
You stand on the shoulders of
titans. Nothing is impossible.

# CHAPTER 1 *LESEDI*

The sun is beginning to rise as it always does. I lay in bed pretending to be asleep, relishing in the golden strips of light heating those parts of my quilt it touches. I did not get much rest last night, or the night before for that matter. I've been too anxious to sleep. I hear Baba in the distance whistling as he prepares his fishing gear for the day. It's always a happy tune. As his footsteps draw nearer, I know I have taken too much time lying in bed.

"I know you are awake, my daughter," Baba says in between tunes as he enters my chambers. The song he so cheerfully whistles seems to be in harmony with the one being sung by the birds outside my window. "How did you know?" I laugh as I pull my quilt over my head.

"A father always knows. The sun is yet to rise, but even the birds sing in the darkness. What is troubling you so early in the morning?"

"Nothing Baba, just tired," I reply convincingly. The truth is I don't really know what is troubling me. Just an uneasy feeling in the pit of my stomach that I can't seem to ignore or rid myself of.

"It is just your nerves in anticipation for tomorrow night's ceremony. The food, the laughter, the dancing! I can hardly wait myself. It will be a beautiful celebration filled with love, family, and music. True Eleguan style!"

That shows how unrested I have been lately. I have almost forgotten about the Feast of the Full Moon. It is one of my most favorite things. Every solstice on the last full moon, we celebrate at night the beauty of darkness. We spend the whole day cooking delicious foods and making flower arrangements. The women braid their hair in interlocking designs adorned with fresh flowers in bright colors. The men paint their faces white, all to symbolize our interwovenness of light and dark. We hang lanterns filled with the sweetest smelling candles all around the village. There is much work and preparation that goes into the Feast of the full Moon. It is all in tribute to the darkness that bloomed the first seed.

The men will be fishing all day tomorrow, while the women head to the market to gather and barter. What the mothers consider barter is more like haggling. It is a good time. All working while happily singing in a distracted anticipation of the feast.

Baba's words always seem to carry truth and love. But that is Baba; always one of joy, positivity, and a little worry. He worries about Mama and me. But Baba is strong, and I trust him. Even still, I can't seem to shake the feeling. But the day must go on. I rise to wash and dress before heading to Mama Oni's hut for a little breakfast before I meet my cousin Nia for our morning lesson.

I step outside of our royal compound to greet the hot morning sun. It is indeed a beautiful day. My deep dark skin absorbs its warmth. The village is already buzzing. Men and women dressed in beautiful wrapped kente cloths and kaftans have begun busying themselves with the day's work. They carry handwoven baskets on their heads and babies on their backs. A few elders are playing a game of mancala with the children left behind while their mamas and babas go to work.

The village is surrounded by flowers and fruit trees. Rows of vegetables and herbs grow nearby. All nourished by the lush river in the valley outside our walls. Inside the walls are the compounds of many families, all arranged in intricate fractal patterns. My family lives together here, adjoined by walls made of red mud bricks. The exterior of each compound is beautifully designed and decorated with those same fractal patterns painted in dazzling colors: greens, blues, reds, and yellows. Inside, each chamber is bright and roomy. Eleguan-made pottery sits on every shelf, and every bed is dressed in quilts that tell the

3

stories of our people.

In the center of our village courtyard is a well, or a pit. Sky Mother provides both fire and water from the center. Our people gather there for everything. Our people gather there for everything, like praying and conducting ceremonies. Feasts, funerals, lectures, and offerings all take place at the sacred center. It is a place of great joy within our village. I take in one more admiring view of the life bustling in front of me before entering Mama Oni's medicine hut. "Good morning, Mama!" I say with a big smile as I enter the snug and sweet-smelling hut.

"Yes, good morning granddaughter" she replies with love. "Come, sit, eat" she says with a warmth and a sternness only a mother could provide. On the table in a shallow wooden bowl, I spot two steaming slices of cooked yam. As I walk to sit, I take in a deep breath that fills my entire chest. I am briefly distracted by the warmth that fills my lungs. Mama Oni's hut smells of delicious food, flowers, and honey. Sunlight pours in the hut windows, bathing plants in large hand painted pots hanging from the windows and ceiling in its pleasant orange glow. I inspect each plant, gently touching with two fingers as I lean in to take a sniff. Mama Oni calls out the names of each one as I round the room.

"Pygeum; used for ailment of the kidneys and stomach. Aloe, notice the red and yellow flowers. Split the leaves, expose the gel, and use it for insect bites, cuts, burns and infections. Devil's claw, to heal pain within the body. Araujia, to heal what ails the mind." I make a mental note of each one, picturing the shapes and colors of the leaves.

Anytime I can get away, I sneak into Mama Oni's hut. I like to spend my mornings here eating yams or cassava while daydreaming. When I get lost in my mind, I think about how I cannot wait to be chief. My name will one day be among the great ancestors. Me, Lesedi Oyebalo, daughter of Chief Lyabo Oyebalo, granddaughter of Chief Mazi Oyebalo, great granddaughter of Chief Nakia Oyebalo. I descend from strong women who have led this village through the ages. Because of them, our land has prospered. Our people are well. For this we give honor to Sky Mother and all the mothers before us for their direction and protection.

I am anxious with anticipation, just thinking about the dreams I hope to inspire. I have so many ideas to share with my people. When I am chief, I will set up a council where I can sit and listen to the dreams of all my people. I dream our Elegua will continue to be profound and magical, filled with the deepest desires of one's own heart that we can share with each other. Much like we have now but better. With more time devoted to exploring and building friendships outside of our village. We will live in eternal bliss and happiness forever. I dream they will call me the *Chief of Dreams*. I'd be a chief, and a healer like my grandmother, Mama Oni. A dreaming healer chief is what I could be. I know much about botany now just from watching her these past 19 years. Mama Oni is 95 years old, and the best healer in the village. It is her gift. Sky Mother blesses us all with special gifts. Mama Oni's is her ability to create without recipes or instructions. All she needs is a sniff or a taste of a plant, and she knows exactly how she can utilize it. Such a wonderful gift she has. I have not yet discovered what exactly my gift is, so I spend a lot of time learning the ways of other's. I find joy in seeing all the many ways many things work together for one.

As my daydreaming continues, I also think about my best friend Kendi, who will arrive later today from the village of Oya. I rarely get to see her. I cannot wait to gossip and exchange stories of all that is happening outside of the walls of our compound. I think about Ukize and his dark shiny skin. It is hard not to get distracted during my staff lessons when Ukize is there glowing regally and looking quite edible. It's the only time I get to see him during the day, as after staff lessons, he joins the rest of the blacksmiths of the village to craft the iron tools and materials needed.

I think about my purpose and what it is Sky Mother wants me to fulfill. Mama Oni likes to tell the story of the beginning of time. I think it is her favorite. It is mine as well. "It is the key to who we are," she always says. She starts by saying in the beginning, there was only Sky Mother. She was deep and powerful. Her vastness composed every space, but she was alone. So, Sky Mother decided to create life. She took fire from her heart and created the sun, so her children could always feel her warmth. She used her tears to create immense waters that would provide nourishment. In her hands she shaped those waters with strands of her hair into a sphere, and Earth was formed. With her breath she breathed on Earth, creating fresh winds that would carry messages to her children. At last, she produced seeds from her womb. She planted these seeds deep in the mud, for only in this dark place could they be nourished to their fullest potential. Where each seed was planted, a lotus flower bloomed. Purple, majestic, and beautiful. It is from those buried seeds we as a people bloomed. Those Lotus flowers marked the land that would become the village of the Elegua, our home, and the home of the great mothers before us. Our people have been on this land since the beginning. We are the descendants of Sky Mother's first children. Our land is sacred. The only place the purple lotus blooms is where the Eleguan dwell.

Each chief is bestowed with the task of protecting the first lotus to ever bloom. It was the first seed Sky Mother planted. It has survived since the beginning of time and is as strong now as it was then. I wonder if that is true for the people of the Lotus. Are we as strong now as we were then when the Earth was new?

In return for the protection the Eleguan provides, the Lotus gives its chief the strength of all the chiefs that provided protection before, making each leader stronger than the last. I look up and Mama Oni smiles and nods in approval, as if she has read my thoughts on my face.

"Lesedi, should you be joining Afua for your lesson, and not daydreaming and wondering about an old woman's hut?" she says with the smallest grin.

"When I am chief, I will cut training time in half to make room for daydreaming," I smile in Oni's direction. Mama Oni smiles back, but I notice her brows furrow.

"Sit down Lesedi, let me tell you something you must know," She moves in close to me and holds my hand in her own. When she looks so deep into my eyes, I feel like she can see my soul.

"You see, Lesedi, we women are born with power, a very intimate and mysterious power. You must learn how to recognize it and control it. If you do not, you will never know your full potential. And if you don't know your full potential, outsiders who can see it will take advantage of you. It is important for you to always remember we women are gifted. It is a wonderous and forceful gift. We are born with a part of Sky Mother's womb, making us divine gatekeepers of her connection to her children. It is our womb itself that gives us our powers. We are empaths, able to detect whatever ails our people, and provide them healing. We birth creation, and restore the cycle of life. That is a heavy load. That is why you must be equipped to carry it. It is so very necessary. That is why we can conjure magic that connects us to nature. We are all one, connected by the circle of life, and with that kind of magic, we can do much light, but also much dark. We must weld it the way Sky Mother intended. That is why she watches over us with a million eyes; stars that can be seen from anywhere in the world. She made her eyes twinkle so bright, so we'd always be able to find our way home anytime we get lost."

"But we never get lost, because we never leave, at least not Eleguan women anyway," I reply with a tone of lazy frustration. I love my land, and I love my people, but I have always longed to see what else Sky Mother created outside our village. Mama Oni's face softens as if she could feel my disappointment. I can tell she knows something I do not.

9

"The rules are only to keep you safe, my daughter. Outside is plagued with war and betrayal. But I must say lately I've been feeling a change in the wind. Yes, the winds are restless," She stops and contemplates for a moment before she continues.

"I must implore you to always remember our foremother's paths are not for us to repeat, but for us to continue, Lesedi. It is very important for you to remember that."

While Mama Oni speaks, she grabs a few herbs hanging from the walls and drops them into an iron pot hanging over the fire. She waves her hand once over top of it, and a purple glow rises like steam. The smell of lavender and chamomile fills the room.

I consider her words for a moment as I inhale the calming smells and stuff my mouth with breakfast. I hope she is right. Can I be the new chief healer to bring my people into a new age of life? Can I start new traditions without neglecting the old? I sometimes wonder how much easier would my life be if I was born a man? Eleguan men cannot conjure magic, for they have no womb, but they are born of Eleguan women, so they are divine, nonetheless. Their magical abilities dwell internally. They have incredible strength and never-ending endurance. They could move mountains from dusk till dawn, and never grow fatigued. In fact, just the opposite. The more they work, the stronger they become. They are known in neighboring villages as callers because of their ability to call to animals. Callers can harness animal instincts as their own, and animals assist them in time of need. Our men are great hunters, but they do not randomly pick and kill, for that is not Sky Mother's way. Instead, they offer blessings to the animals in return for their sacrifice. The animals they bless become their spirit animals, linking their likeness to ours. When we die, we feed our bodies become the earth that feeds the animals. This is Sky Mother's will. We are all connected.

Baba is the best Caller in the village. His animal instincts are so strong, he need only encounter an animal once, and he can use their powers as his own forever. Baba once harnessed the strength and the memory of an elephant. In return, he blessed the elephant with the gift of triumph over all enemies who came to hunt him for his ivory. When Baba calls to animals, they hear him, and they seek him. Baba once made an offering to Sky Mother, asking her to bless the fish with abundance, which she did. We Eleguan believe that what will benefit one will benefit all. In return, every day when our men go to the river to fish, the fish present them with a sacrifice of the fattest one in their school.

Because Eleguan men's powers lie within their strength, and not their magic, they can travel anywhere. But not ours. Our women can only conjure magic on our sacred land. So, every day the men go out to fish, hunt, gather wood, and sell goods at the market. Our women work within the village as teachers, healers, priestesses, and diplomats. They take counsel within the village, meeting with people from near and far, listening to their frustrations and misfortunes.

I often consider following the men when they leave the village walls. I did it often when I was young, but Baba caught me and returned me himself. Ever since then, the entire village watches me like a hawk. I sense they feel the desperate need to protect their wandering future chief. Mama is the chief of our village. She is strict but fair. Many people travel long journeys to hear what they call *Chief Lyabo's divine wisdom*. Mama doesn't smile much unless Baba is around, but her smile is beautiful. Her skin is chestnut brown, just like her long locs that when untied dance down her back. Her eyes are almond shaped, slanted, and all knowing. Mama decides which causes are just enough for Sky Mother's blessing. Sky Mother does not adhere to selfish requests that benefit only one. *We are because I am, and I am because we are*. That is Sky Mother's will.

Mama deals with the most serious issues. Once, a chief from

the Oya village came to Mama complaining of a dark spirit that was plaguing their land, scaring away the livestock and causing crops to wither and die. The Oya people were in danger of not having any harvest to last them through the season. Mama consulted with Baba's mama, Mama Oni, and her closest advisor, Abeena. Together, they gathered the council of elders and set up an altar to pray. On the alter, there were offerings of shark fish, fresh greens, oils, amethyst, and palm wine. Sky Mother then sent a recipe for a healing tonic through the wind straight to Mama Oni. Baba and the elder men gathered the plants and herbs. It took them two days to find them all. Mama and seven other elders prayed, mixed, and chanted incantations over the tonic all night. In the morning, Mama and the elders drank, giving them special healing powers within their magic that the Oya people needed for their land, and making certain their magic would sustain them during the journey.

When Mama and the women elders arrived in Oya, they blessed each family in the village individually, ensuring wellness and prosperity. But most importantly, they gave the mental gift of empathy; the ability to love your neighbor as you love yourself. Now the Oya people bring us offerings once every full moon to thank us for their prosperity. Their messenger is a girl my age named Kendi. She is my best friend. I envy her freedom to roam. I ask Kendi about the different places she has traveled. She speaks excitedly as she recounts stories of befriending lions in the jungle and eating fruit in the trees with gorillas. We laugh at the wild embellishments. Truthfully, women have less freedom in her village than we do here. The men seem to decide what their women should wear and whom they shall marry. She is envious that Eleguan women create their own destiny, even if it is within the walls of our village.

Today Kendi will arrive. I always wait for her at the bottom of the hill along the river that leads to our valley. When she arrives at the top of the hill, I see a curvy silhouette with long black wool-like hair flowing upwards like tidal waves in the wind. Kendi is always barefoot. She squishes the grass between her toes as she walks, picking lotus flowers along the river as she approaches. I wish I could see her village and learn her ways and her songs. But I must stay here and train. My mind wonders, imagining all the places I would go if I was Kendi. I'm so in awe of them all, I almost don't notice Mama as she enters Mama Oni's hut.

"Lesedi, I knew I'd find you here. Afua informed me that you did not show up for the staff lesson you were to take before dawn in place of the lesson you missed last week."

I tried to smile while I thought of how to plead my case, but quickly abandoned the idea at the sight of Mama's blazing eyes.

"Should a future chief not know how to defend herself and her people?" Mama asked fiercely as she made her entrance into the tiny hut.

"I am sorry Mama, I lost track of time."

"You are gifted with the staff, but lazy in your training, Lesedi. That is unacceptable."

I tried to hide my eyes and caught a glimpse of Mama Oni trying to hide a smile.

"I will have to mention to the elders that they must keep a closer eye on you, my daughter. You have the wanderer spirit like your father. I've sensed it on you since your birth. You are 19 now, and one day you will take my place as chief, and you must be ready."

"I know Mama, I will go now."

As I gather myself to leave, I hear Mama say in a rushed voice "Mama Oni your presence is urgently requested. An Oyan messenger has arrived, but it is not the girl. A man who calls himself Masozi has arrived in her place. He claims he has been wrongfully cursed by Sky Mother and demands a blessing. We must hold counsel immediately."

"How can that be when each Oyan home was blessed individually?" asks Mama Oni.

"He says his home skipped."

# CHAPTER 2 *MASOZI*

As I wait for the chief to return with her council, I cannot help but look around. Such humble abodes for such spoiled people. They can create whatever they please, yet they choose to give more than they receive. *Foolish Eleguan.* I catch my reflection in a basin of water. My face is covered in fatigue and frustration. I splash the water, attempting to wash the tiredness away. When I open my eyes, the Chief is before me with seven members of her council.

"Chief Lyabo, I am Masozi of the Oya Village, and I have come to collect what Sky Mother owes me."

"What offering do you bring for Sky Mother?"

"I bring none." I replied frostily. "What offering does Sky Mother have for me?"

She looks at me with an expression that I cannot read. It angers me. The look of pity that I know too well always seems to trigger my resentment for life.

"I have been cursed since birth for my father's sins. My mother abandoned our home when I was a small child. My father then turned to palm wine to drown his sorrows, leaving our field of yams and me neglected. He squanders our money at the market on his own happiness. I, in return, am forced to tend to the field alone and sell what little we have at the market. My field is often overgrown, hiding us from the rest of the village, and I cannot afford a wife to help with the labor our land requires." The council before me exchanged looks between them, as if they can read one another's mind. The chief then turns to me to speak.

"I have consulted with the council, and it seems as though you are correct in your claim to the Great Blessing. It is a mistake that can be corrected. In two days' time, we shall have what we need—»

"No. I do not request a blessing of prosperity over my home. That was never a home to me. No, instead I ask for riches: diamonds, gold, and rubies. I wish to leave the life I was cursed to have and live spoiled until my end. That is my right. I shall afford a beautiful wife and leave the life of a yam farmer behind me."

"I see," the chief responds with a look I cannot discern.

"I am sorry, but I am afraid I must deny your request. For no one will benefit from increased riches, including yourself. Your greed will only bring more jealousy, envy, and death, and that is not Sky Mother's way. *We are because I am, and I am because we are.* Sky Mother only blesses us with gifts that will bless others. That is her way."

The Chief's word hit hard with a finality. Rage overwhelms me. Those recurring feelings of anger, sadness, and hopelessness settle into my bones and make themselves at home. Once again, my endeavors have failed. I cannot stop the words from spewing. "You Eleguan are foolish! Sheltered here in your huts when a whole world of riches is right at your feet. When I take what Sky Mother owes me, I shall build castles in my name. People will pray to me instead of Sky Mother. They will come for a share of my vast riches, and I, the true benign one, will bless them. They shall serve me forever, you will see."

Consumed in my own darkness, I storm out into the harshness of the sunshine. As I descend over the big hill east of the valley, the daunting reality of having to return to that forsaken farm starts to engulf me. My frustration cannot be contained as I cry aloud. "Curse you, Sky Mother! You have brought me only pain. What have I done to deserve such a life? To suffer the abandonment of a mother, and the drunkenness of a father. Do I not deserve compensation for my plight? I am a good man. My hands are calloused from my days of working in the fields. Yet I remain poor! And those selfish, spoiled Eleguan turn their noses up at me, and refuse to bless *me*. One day I shall have all the Motherland's riches. I shall not stop. From this day on I am a farmer no more. From this day forward I shall take what is rightfully mine."

"Why steal? I can supply you with riches beyond your wildest dreams. You need just ask."

The sound of the voice sends a wave of fear through me. I recognize the language. It was not my own, but I was familiar with it from trading and doing business at the merchant stands closest to the ocean shores. I turned my head around so quickly my vision blurred. I find a man in a peculiar dress, covered in shiny metal. His face is the color of cream. His eyes, though blue as the sky, seem to harness a fire.

"Who are you?"

"I am Captain Christopher Dias. I am an explorer and merchant looking to trade with new friends, and I come bearing gifts. The same gifts I couldn't help but overhear you wish to steal. I only require one gift from you in return."

The man called Christopher Dias reaches into his pocket and pulls out a small leather pouch. He unties it and watches me with the tiniest hint of a smirk as my eyes seem to carry my feet into this tiny bag of sparkling white and silver stones that twinkle like stars. I do not speak. I cannot speak, for my body has been hypnotized by what lies before me. I listen intently as the captain continues, never breaking my line of sight to the leather pouch.

"I need men and women to take along my journey with me. If you can provide me with quality captives, I shall reward you with this very satchel."

I smile as a plan quickly formulates in my head. How much richer I could be with the captain's diamonds and the Eleguan's magic. My mouth curls into a devilish smile.

"It is a deal."

It doesn't take long for a plan to begin to form in my mind. The feast of the full moon will take place in two days' time. The men will rise early to begin fishing and trading in the market. All in preparation for the celebration. I know their complete morning routine, as I once followed them every day for a fortnight in hopes of stealing some of their premium catches. I cannot afford their fish in the market. I instead eat less than perfect yams from my garden. The best yams I save to be sold. I know the men cannot be trapped in nets, and will tear through it easily. And the men cannot be chased, as they are too fast, moving with catlike speed. I will have to subdue them with a special herb that grows from a red flower deep within the jungle and paralyzes the body. When ingested, the body will have no choice but to succumb to a full day of sleep. We will raid the village during their slumber and put all the Eleguan in chains. When they awaken, we will tell them they have been drained of their powers. Once they believe their powers have been stripped, their minds will enter a stage of hopelessness. When their women seek to find them, we shall capture them too. I diverge from the path home and head deep into the jungle. I must find that herb. I have sweet yams to prepare.

# CHAPTER 3 *LESEDI*

I met my cousin Nia before our morning lesson. We share a few whispers before Ife, a strong and stocky boy from our village arrives. Nia and Ife are in the silliest type of love. They laugh and giggle and stare into each other's eyes all day. Auntie Abeena says they are both so silly in love that they will probably walk right into the river smiling and holding hands. Ife knows all the ways to make Nia smile. They exchange a few quick glances and many long gazes, followed by a few sickening words that show how much they really love each other.

"Let me help you with that, your hands should not touch the ground," Ife says after Nia drops her leather pouch on the ground, so obviously purposely.

"Oh, Ife thank you for your kindness," Nia replies sweetly, blinking her eyelashes. "You will someday make a wife so thankful to have such a thoughtful husband." They gazed into each other's eyes with silly grins on their faces, looking like two lovestruck hyenas.

While Nia and Ife gape and swoon, I quietly sit and wait in the back for Ukize, a man so fine, I cannot help but stare. His skin is so dark, it glows like the fur of the panther he becomes when he is transformed into his spirit animal. He is strong from his work as a blacksmith's apprentice and the hunting he does with his father and the other men in the village. His dark muscles are wide and defined. He is so tall, his shoulders seem to touch the sky. His hands and feet are big, and his voice is as low as a growl. I love the way he says my name so slowly and long: Lesedi, carefully pronouncing each syllable. He will be my husband one day. I am sure of it. I make sure to put on a little extra lotus oil when I know that he's going to be around. He walks in, and I meet his gaze. It seems as if he approaches in the slowest of motions. He smiles and greets me with a short bow, which I return. He says in a growl of a whisper with a grin "Lesedi, you smell of only the sweetest flowers and the freshest herbs, good enough to eat," his deep voice vibrating.

I blush and respond "My Ukize, whenever you are hungry, I shall feed you," with a smile he returns so warmly. I try to remember that I must always remain proper, for I am the future chief, but for now, I am young and in love. Who says a chief cannot be both?

In our village, men and women train together. We are like one big family. We all help and look out for each other, but most importantly, we share our gifts together. Everyone contributes to the community, and everyone plays a role. It starts from the time a child is even thought of. When a young woman is ready to conceive, she goes to see the elders. The elders will pray for the child's journey from the spiritual realm to the physical realm. When the prayer is complete, she will meet with Mama Oni. Then, Mama Oni and Zuri, our village midwife, will go into the woods and get the leaves and herbs needed to make the tea for her womb. The tonic ensures the baby's health and comfort will sustain. Nine months later, a baby is born. Those babies grow into the children whose laughter and jubilance make for the best of days. One of the roles of the children is to pick all the fruit and distribute it to the village. They like to climb high in the trees to get to the fruit way at the top. Because they cannot see what fruit the tree holds from the ground, the children identify the trees by their fragrance. We learn here in Elegua to trust all our senses, not just our sense of sight. What we hear, smell and feel can also guide us.

When a child in the village turns ten years old, they begin their training.

The boys in the village will accompany the men on their daily chores. Everything they learn is a lesson in how to survive. They don›t learn how to hunt or how to fight right away. First, they must learn how to read the terrain around them with every one of their senses; how to see what›s around them without being seen themselves. How to read the

Earth with their hands, feeling for tracks that will tell the story of the previous traveler; how to identify what plants are edible and which are not by watching how to pick and taste wild greens; how to mark their paths by breaking the branches and arranging them in a way that will aid them in finding their way home.

Once they have mastered all those skills, only then will the fathers then take the boys out to hunt.

Those same skills learned in the wild can be applied to society. I am the future chief, so I am well-versed in all that must be learned, and despite my daydreaming, I excel. Training is as much a lesson in oneness among us as it is preparation for war. We don›t look for war, but we keep our army strong, so we are always prepared to defend ourselves against outsiders who look to go to war with us. But the elders have become increasingly worried about the stories of kidnapping and violence we keep hearing about on the outside. Whispers fill the market with stories of raids, killings, and pillaging. Mama and Baba have done well to keep an extra eye on me since then. I've been finding it hard to sneak away and enjoy the sunset behind the savannah from a hill in the valley with Ukize. It is our secret spot, but lately, it is getting harder and harder for us to get time alone together.

I spend my day as I usually do. Warrior training with my staff, followed by lessons in history and etiquette in the morning, herb picking and cooking in the midday, then dinner with the family in the evening. Dinner is filled with laughter and the delicious smells of rice and lamb. After a few songs and some dancing with the kids of the village around the sacred center, I finally wash up and get ready for bed.

That night, I laid awake waiting for the darkest part of night that is calm and still. The only sounds are owls hooting and crickets chirping off in the distance. I'm worried about Kendi. She's my best friend. I know she would never choose to miss out on an afternoon of laughs and storytelling and a little gossip too. I hope she is well. Mama and the elders haven't put much thought into why she had not come. They're more troubled by the messenger that came in her place. I overheard Mama say to Afua his spirit disturbed her, as it was one of the most troubled she had felt in many moons. I bet he knows why Kendi did not come. If she is in trouble, she will need our powers to save her. I need to speak to this troubled messenger of Oya. It is urgent. But Mama would never allow it. Maybe I can convince Baba to let me accompany him to the river today, then I can sneak off to the market, full of Oyan farmers. I will say it is my job as future chief to know the work of all my people, but I know what he will say in return. I would plead my best argument saying "Baba, I think something bad may have happened to Kendi. It is unlike her to miss a trip to our village. I think it is my duty as future chief to accompany the men to the market today, you know, for political purposes. Plus, I think the farmer from her village may know what has happened to her. And it is my duty as future chief to know the work of all my people." My eyes would plead with his, but his eyes would only look back into mine with pity.

"I am sorry my love." He would say. "You know if I did that what your mother would say. That woman scares me sometimes." Then Baba would smile, but I would hang my head. Then he'd say "Lesedi, we all have a place. Yours, for now, is here where it is safe. You know, your mother always says you've got my wanderer spirit. I've always known that, ever since you were a baby. You are destined to do great things, my love. Do not rush it, your time will come. I've seen you with a staff, I would not be surprised if it was Sky Mother's plan for you to be the greatest of defenders." Thinking back to the words I've heard so many times confirms that I know exactly what I must do.

Slowly, I rise and wrap myself in a robe made of the softest silk. I neglect my shoes, opting instead to feel the cold earth beneath my feet. I grab a candle, some fruit and a goblet of wine for an offering, and head out into the velvety purple night sky. The stars all seem to be shining on me. I see reflections of their glow on my dark brown skin, as if Sky Mother had every eye one me, watching me as I walked through the darkness.  The cool night winds blow my long afro of curls into my face. In the courtyard is the sunken garden that holds the sacred well. It sits on a circle platform of white marbled stone circled by a shallow basin that collects water from the rain. When I finally reached the landing of the basin, I light my candle and set it down. Around it I arrange flowers from the sunken garden, and the fruit and wine I carried with me. I kneel and begin to pray.

"Sky Mother, creator of Earth. Our protector and provider. I come first to say thank you for your love and guidance, and the abundance I have been fortunate to live among. I know it has been the way of mothers before me to stay within our village. It is how we have stayed safe and avoided the wars that have plagued our neighbors. But I feel it is my duty to leave. Please forgive me for not following the paths set for me. I feel the universe around me urging me to run. I keep wondering what life is. What is the purpose and the meaning? Why are we here? Sometimes I think I've found the answer in the things I love. Life is the warm light of the sun, but also the trees that provide shade from it. The concept of duality that exists in nature captivates me. The idea that opposing factors often provide definition and clarity to what is misunderstood is fascinating to me. Are we here to enjoy our days in solitude with the ones we love, or are we meant to be opposed? Will opposition reveal our true purpose? Do we know who we truly are if we don't know what we're opposed to? Of course, I don't have the answers, Sky Mother, but I like to think of all the possibilities on early summer mornings as I lay awake in bed, watching the sunrise in the East and listening to the calls of the birds who rise with it. When my mind wonders, it reminds me of the disruption a ripple can cause to the still water. How a small stone can cause an endless wave. I like to think of myself as that small stone. I know you already know , Sky Mother, that I cause enough disruptions within our tribe. Mama says I must stop daydreaming and prepare to be chief. It is the strength of our women that has carried us this far and it is up to me to continue that legacy. I hope to be the kind of chief that can show my people we can do more now than we ever have before. We can expand, we can build and network with neighboring tribes. Of course, Mama won't hear of it. If it doesn't follow tradition, it is not Sky Mother's way, Mama always says. Yet, still I long to be a chief of duality. So, I am here, Sky Mother, to ask you to bless me and guide me as I set out on a new journey. I don't know where it will lead me, but I trust that you will be there."

When my prayer is complete, I blow out the candle. Leaving the offering behind me, I glide on the wind as it leads me back to my bed. Feelings of both calm and frenzy circle in my stomach like butterflies as the sound of the night rocks me to sleep.

The next day, I awaken early to put my plan in motion. I pray first, and then I am on my way. From my secret stash, I grab seeds of herbs gathered from Mama Oni's hut. In my braids, I hide the herb seeds along rice, red pepper, and okra seeds. Just in case, I'm gone longer than intended. I dress in dark brown linens that cover my hair and neck. I move inconspicuously as I follow the path that leaves my village. Only looking behind me once to capture a last glimpse of the colorful fractals, I am headed to the market to find the Oyan messenger.

The path there leads me past the river where Baba and the other men fish. I must stay quiet and stay hidden, careful not to be detected by their animal instincts.

From a distance, I notice a beggar pushing a cart filled with what looks like jars of whipped sweet yams. He offers them to the men, in return for one fish. I watch the exchange from a distance. The men take a break from the hot sun and gather under a tree at the riverbank to enjoy a sweet snack. Then suddenly all at once, the men drop to their sides. I rush off, panic washing over me. As quickly as I can, I run back to my village. Time and my lungs seem to both be standing still, as my feet do the work my mind can't seem to do. I rush through the village walls straight to our compounds, not stopping until I reach Mama's chambers. "Mama, Mama! Please come quick!" I yell frantically as I barge though the hut where the council of women meet. "It is the men!

Something has happened, I think they've been poisoned!"

"Lesedi!" Mama looks at me with wild eyes, then at two of her most trusted advisors, Abeena on her right and Afua on her left.

"Gather the women," She says in a voice that is both calm and terrifying. Abeena blows a horn made from the antlers of an antelope.

All at once, the feet are heard moving in unison. In no time, the women appear, looking war -ready and possessed. Staffs and machetes in hand, Mama leads as we all run back to the river. We run like no tomorrow until we reach the hill that leads to the valley of the riverbank. Then suddenly, out of nowhere the sound of a million thunders erupts around me. Fire shoots through the air, hitting Zuri in her chest. Blood flows like water, and she drops to the ground. The women move with stealth, but they are no match for the invisible bombs. One by one, I watch bodies drop around me. Smoke clouds the airs. Then everything goes dark.

# CHAPTER 4 *MASOZI*

The sun was violently hot that morning. It seemed to have been burning down upon the Earth with a vengeance. The men with skin the color of cream sat on a hill, their faces red and covered in sweat and their eyes filled with a terrifying hunger. Held straight out in front of them were long metal pipes that shot fire. I watched from a distance, anxious at last for the defeat of the Eleguan, the greedy people who think they are above the rest of us. The women warriors then appear suddenly and silently. In uniform formations with weapons branding, they charge for the outsiders on the hill. Boom! Boom! Fire rang out recklessly in all directions. Blood watered the ground until some were dead, and others lay too injured or too afraid to move. The remaining women join their men and lie face down on the earth. The ghostlike faces quickly descend upon them and tie them like cattle, making sure to explore their bodies with their hands as they do so. Slowly they are led off into the harshness of the sun, leaving only footprints in the earth behind them.

After the Eleguan are successfully captured, I continue to bargain with the Europeans, raiding village after village. I now have more riches than I ever knew what to do with. My ascent to royalty will need some planning of course. I will need to establish a following and a place to dwell. Naturally I will take what was formally Elegua as mine now that that problem had been eradicated. It will take much doing, but I will get to that part later. In the meantime, I travel to the market every day. I purchase silk robes, massive shark fish and plums. Now when I go to the market it doe not sell yams. Life is finally comfortable. My yard is still overgrown, and Baba is sleeping more, as there is now more palm wine than one man could ever drink in a day. Some days I will lose Baba completely, as he will pass out in the fields, and I will be unable to find him until he awakens from his drunkenness and groan in the dark for more. I know I will have to leave this place soon. I decide next that I will look for a wife. It will be the first thing I did in the morning. How am I to know that the morning will never come? How am I to know that in the night they will come; that in the night, I too would become a victim snatched and shackled, stripped of my satchel of riches, my dignity, and my pride, and made to walk the muddy clay roads to my demise?

The sky turns angry. Dark, with rain, thunder, and lightning. It is as if Sky Mother's fury is swallowing the land. I can hardly breathe as we approach a stark white castle, the smell of salt and decay lingering in the wetness of the air. As I descend into the castle, I am now sure that Sky Mother has inflicted punishment upon me. I spot the captain Dias in the distance. He smiles at me with all the charm of a serpent. My frustration cannot be contained as I scream violently in anger. I am hit with a crushing blow, and everything goes dark. I am awake, just unable to open my eye.

We walk the long path down into the dungeons. We have to crouch low to fit in down the cold, clammy, and bloody narrow halls. We are forced together in a dark, dank doom. I am naked on the cold earth surrounded by other men who look defeated. I lie awake in my chains thinking about Baba. How will he buy his palm wine without me? There is little harvest left, and the fields needs extensive tending. Will he survive? Will he miss me? Will he notice that I'm gone? I think of the diamonds and the gold that was mine for only a fortnight. I think about the day the captain named Dias came to me. I was a fool to trust him.

The dungeon of the castle smells of dead animal carcasses. I'm surrounded by many men, some of them the Eleguan that I sacrificed for my better life, which I had the luxury to live for only the briefest moment. I don't know what awaits us, but I am certain it is only disaster. The magic I resented lingers on my mind, as I can't help but think how ironic it is that only that magic can save us now. I wonder if Mama was here what she would say? Did she always know I was unsuitable to be a son? Is that why she left? My thoughts are interrupted as a creek from the dungeon door sends a crack of light through. The men with Dias holding us captive lead us one by one to the deck of a massive ship. They parade us around exposed as they examine our manhood. They make words in their language that sound like 'valuable' and 'nigger'. The feeling of guilt, fear, anger, and shame swirl around in my stomach and threatens to bring up what has been burning in my stomach. Chief Lyabo was right about my selfish desires. I have caused death and destruction at the hands of the most terrible beings. I will honor Sky Mother from this moment on, as I know death must be near.

# CHAPTER 5 *LESEDI*

I cannot believe my eyes. I am completely frozen in terror. Something unimaginable is ravaging through us. How could an evil like this exist? How could Sky Mother allow this? Why has she not yet rained down with a vengeance? We are held in a dungeon for days. I hear the sounds of waves crashing outside the walls. The feeling of sorrow encapsules me like the shell of a clam. It freezes me in time. I cannot eat or think or dream. There is only pain. Flashbacks of fire booming and blood spilling. It is like my body is not mine. I am like a ghost, numb and hollow as I am led to a ship bigger than I've ever seen, chained from head to toe.

On the boat, we are led to the lowest deck where no light comes through. White men come down here often and pick us out one by one. Women return looking like their souls have been taken from them. And then it hits me, a sharp pain in my chest like a knife. As light creeps in, I see Kendi in the corner, eyes wide open and not blinking, dirty, and bleeding. Her breast exposed, and her stare vacant. I scream her name, but I cannot move. In the creep of that white light, I see covered feet approach me. A single key unlocks me, and I know my fate will soon be matched with Kendi's as I am led to the white face's chamber.

When I am returned, I am chained again on my hands and feet. Blood escaping my body. We sleep on the floor of the vessel; shoulder to shoulder, feet to head, and head to feet. Any way they could make us fit. We're packed like dead shark fish on our way to be sold to the highest bidder.

I do not know how much time has passed. I have not seen Mama. I cannot get to Kendi. I need to tell her I am here. I need to lie to her when I comfort her by telling her we will be okay. Kendi is seldom chained in the bottom with us. I saw her that day they brought us to the deck. Half-dead and chained with a rope that extended from the shackle around her neck and led to the white fingers of the monster holding it. My stomach threatens to spill over as my eyes lock with hers. All that she cannot say seeks me, and I'm filled with horror.

The only time we are unchained is when they yell and tell us to dance and entertain them. We're beaten with whips if we refuse. They unlock our shackles and remove our chains as they stand around and watch with hungry eyes as our feet and hands begin to move rhythmically.

We chant our prayers as we dance. They don't understand us or our language, so they laugh and clap and pass a bottle of clear wine among them while we sing our pains and prayers to Sky Mother above. Amid the chant, I hear my name.

"Lesedi," I whip around to find Mama is behind me, still dancing, not making eye contact, but now closely whispering so only I can hear her under the singing and chanting.

"Mama!"

"Shh, I don't have much time. Listen, Lesedi, I have taught you all I could, but I can go with you no further, it is not my path. I am not meant to make the journey towards the western sun, but you must go on. Take this with you and guard it with your life. It is key," Mama reached in her long locced hair and pulled out a single purple lotus flower which she then quickly tucked inside my tight coiled hair.

"I will always be with you, but this is where I leave you."

And then I heard it. Before I could give my Mama the proper goodbye, out rang the war cry of my people. Mama and Abeena jump into action, grabbing a pole holding a flag and swinging it as if it were a staff. Afua in the distance delivers a swift kick to the face of a white man, and she grabs the hand of her young son. It's as though they walked right up to the sun, hand in hand, as the two bodies plunged deep into the dark water below. And from the corner of my eye, I saw Mama approach the edge. She dives with precision as her slender body hits the water. Mama takes in a mouth full of water, inhaling Sky Mother's salty tears and embracing her descent into the ocean, slowly rejoining with the circle of life. The white men are back with the fire shooting poles. I can't stand the sound of it. Like earthquakes. We are rushed back to the bottom deck and again covered in darkness.

I'm weary with the ways of the world. The waves outside made me sick. That, mixed with a vision of Mama plunging in the dark blue waters brings something up from my stomach. I don't know what because I have not eaten in days besides the beans I was forced fed who knows how long ago. Some of us captives refuse to eat in protest. We were then met with a tool used for removing teeth, and told they had no problem shoving food down our throats. What are they trying to keep us alive for? After that day Mama jumped, they started shackling us together two by two so that we couldn't run or try to plot together.

The days and nights run as one here. Laying still, I throw up covering myself in vile. I lay in it for days, numb. Kalisha, a girl from my village, no older than 12 or 13 is next to me. Her womb bleeds for six days. For six days, I feel the warmth of her blood as it flows from her and drips down my backside. After a while, I can't tell the difference between her blood and my sweat. I want so desperately to be unchained, to swim with Mama and the shark fish. But I am chief now and these are my people chained around me. I make it a point to stay close to Kalisha, hold her hand sometimes and squeeze it, so she knows I'm still here. Especially at night when the men with white faces ravage through our women. I hear their screams, but I can't protect them. We hear our men on a lower deck, separated from us. We hear them weep, unable to protect us, and not knowing the fate of their women and children. For months we live in this hell, halfway dead, until one day the boat stops, and it occurs to me the hell I leave behind me on that forsaken ship also awaits me in this forsaken land.

# CHAPTER 6 *LESEDI*

I didn't know what would await me on the other side. I knew an unimaginable evil was among us, but no one could have pictured a monster of this magnitude. The evil men rush us off the boat, still chained and bleeding, stinking, and covered in vile and waste. From one side of doom to another.

The port is busy with people of every color bustling around dressed in strange clothing. People who look like me, both in chains and walking free. I look around once more to see my people crying. Their faces etched with looks of panic. Mamas separated from their babies, and husbands separated from their wives. It's all too much. Everywhere I look I see horror. Even when I look inside of me.

My people are stripped, rinsed down with buckets of icy water, and assessed like cattle. They count our teeth and grope our bodies. One by one, we wait for a most certain doom. My mind feels like it's breaking. Flashbacks of Mama diving into the ocean, and the smell of the white man's breath as he tore through my body. Suddenly, I feel something come over me. And then, all at once, the wind turns cold, and the sky turns purple. I close my eyes and open my palms to the dark sky. My fingers buzz. This power is one I've never harnessed, but how familiar it feels. Is this magic? But how, so far from home? The lotus buried deep beneath the coils of my hair is warm. My scalp tingles. It feels as if majestic energy is flowing from my head throughout my veins. *I have magic.* I open my eyes. One sharp move of my hand and a bolt of lightning hits with a booming thunder, sparking a fire in a tree. Panic arises. Another wave of my hand, and a purple bolt strikes down with vengeance, hitting a wagon and setting it instantly a blaze. The burning tree snaps and hits the ground, barely missing a group of pale-faced spectators. Chaos erupts. Fire is everywhere, but the wind is cold. My hands, as I look down, are wrapped in a purple glow. Lightning continues to strike, sending slave buyers in a frenzy, grabbing my people by their chains and running for cover. It is at that very moment that I realized my chains are gone. Hot melted iron drips into the earth. I look around. In this distance I see thick forests covered in vegetation right before facing a swamp. Without hesitation, I run. I run like I've never run before; like my life depends on it. *It does.* Into the woods, I am an unstoppable force. Branches break beneath my feet. It all hits me at once, Mama, Baba, the ship, Kendi. I am so afraid; so sad and so broken. I just keep running; I run until I can run no more. The sky is still purple. My feet are bleeding. I feel my power draining as the cold wind soothes me. Sweat drips into my eyes, I'm blinded by it *all*. Collapsing into the leaves, panic starts to set in. I untie my long braids. thick coils warm my shoulders as a bush of hair falls. I reach beneath my hair and remove the flower. The lotus is intact, not a petal missing. I put it back to my scalp and braid one long braid down the center, securing it in place. I'm hungry and I'm cold, but I cannot move. Drained, I'm bound to the Earth by an invisible force. My eyes betray me as my heavy lids surrender. As I drift into a dream, I hear leaves crunching in the distance, and maybe humming? A soothing song. I should run, but the smooth humming carries me into a dream.

I find myself in some kind of abyss. Mama sits on a finely crafted rug cross legged, surrounded by an amber glow.

"Mama?"

"My daughter," Mama replies with a smile and a voice so warm, it instantly relaxes me. What a journey you've been on, and it has only just begun." My cheeks feel the hot sting of my tears, but I cannot speak. I am transfixed by the divinity that is my Mama.

"I am here to remind you to always remember who you are; Always remember our principles; *Always remember our stories*. Let them be a guide to you. As you journey through the valley of the shadow of death, fear no evil. We are with you, your foremothers before you are all here. Remember the ways of your staff. Remember the peaceful shepherd who used his staff to protect his sheep in the time of danger. When you are alone, prepare a table with oils and herbs, and your lotus. We will meet you there."

"Mama, I can't. I lost Baba and I.. I.." I cannot hardly finish, overwhelmed by my own anxiety I freeze in the realization that my reality has forever changed.

"Listen to me, Lesedi, you *must* always believe you can. That is imperative. The key to our power is knowing that we have it. You are strong! You are of Sky Mother herself! Respect her and yourself by remembering your name! Go on, we will lead you from the stars."

I watch Mama become the amber glow, as it bursts with life and disappears, leaving me alone in the dark abyss. I hear it again, the humming. It reminds me of my Baba early in the morning when I would pretend to still be sleeping just to hear him sing. I'm afraid to open my eyes.

# CHAPTER 7 *CHIEF RUNNING BULL*

Her mind struggles, but her body lays motionless. She's hot to the touch, as if fire itself runs through her veins. Beneath her thick hair is a lavender glow. It forms a luminescent crown. She carries the lotus flower. She is the one the ancestors showed me in a dream. But how? So much power was not meant to be harnessed by one person: a girl, barely a woman at that. I lean over her so she can see my face.

"I'm going to help you now, but it is not safe here, so I will advise you keep your voice to a whisper," Her voice takes shape in a deadly tone.

"Who are you, and what do you want? Tell me now! How is it that you have me bound with no ties?"

"I will answer all of your questions, but we must leave now."

"I will find my own way."

"It is not me that has you bound. I know you carry the sacred flower.

It is stronger than you know. It has drained you. You've traveled far and are unwell. Without my help, they will find you and they will kill you, or *worse*. We must keep the lotus safe. I will care for you until you are ready to run again." A crack of sunlight parts through the trees and lights a path. The same light reflects in the flower bearer›s eyes as she studies the path made clear by the sun. She looks at me with wild eyes, like an owl›s in the night.

"What is your name, gatekeeper?"

"My name is Chief Running Bull, descendant of Western Earth. It is nice to meet you, flower bearer, descendent of Eastern Earth."

She replies "I am Lesedi..." in a hushed tone. She stops as if she has misspoken, then clears her throat as if she has suddenly remembered. "*Chief* Lesedi," she says with conviction.

"Let us go now, time is of the essence."

I close my eyes and let the transformation take place. I feel my body contort, while I feel my strength increase. When I feel my horns protrude, I know the transformation is complete. The flower bearer locks her eyes on me as they dance in a frenzy of fascination.

"You are magic," she says with a satisfied and appreciative smile.

"All of us descendants of Earth are, though in different ways. Hop on princess and hold on tight."

We take off in a dash of light. I run fast, maybe the fastest I ever have. For a moment the wind is so soothing I almost forget about the daunting task at hand, almost. Finally, we arrive at a small domelike hut, hidden between large trees and wild branches. *Home.* I feel my back straighten and my fingers return as I transform back to my human form. Lesedi is weak and looks as if she may faint any minute. I quickly helped her down to a pile of quilts on top of the animal hide floor. In a makeshift pit, I make a fire and lower my kettle for tea. When I look over again, the princess is sleeping.

For three days, she lay sick in and out of sleep, sweaty, and feverish, recovering from the long journey and the conditions she'd inhabited over the last few months. I keep fresh herbs steaming around her and place healing stones in her hands while she sleeps. Citrine and quartz in one hand, fluoride and onyx in the other. On the fourth day, she awakened. Tea for me, but for the princess, a tonic to enhance her natural strengths. I spot two clay mugs made by my people. I hand her one. She looks at the piece of pottery as though there is a sad memory attached. *How does she know?* How could she know that my memories of my people would soon be her own? I grind the herbs and pour the water. The warmth of the drinks instantly brings a glow to our faces. Her eyes are too heavy for a woman so young. Those brown omniscient eyes are carrying the burdens of the world. And she is scared.

"May I ask you a few questions? she asks meekly.

"Of course," I reply.

"Well first... Where am I?

"You are in the lands West of the Atlantic."

"Do you know a way for me to get home from here?

"No, not as of yet, but I will tell you what you need to know to survive here."

I notice as she leans in her eyes harness a look of urgency, ready to take in as much knowledge as possible. I continue, making sure to be precise in my wording.

"Our core values make us who we are, but they do not exist without their opposites. How will you know triumph if you do not know failure? How will you know security if you do not know insecurity? Day and night cannot dwell together, but how will you know light if you do not know dark? As you have learned, there are evils in this world. Evils that seek to destroy you. These evils will define you by showing you what you are not. So, the question is, Princess, *what* will you be in opposition to evil? This land has been infested with the spirit of greed. Our sky mothers and fathers give abundantly, there is no need for greed. Greed is human made and the result of its opposite; benevolence- which is divinely made. Greed is the destroyer of all things, unlike benevolence which is the creator of all things. But how would we know one without the other?

I stop for a moment to make sure my words are not lost on her. They are not. Even now in a land so unfamiliar to her, she exudes the coolness and fierceness needed to be a leader amongst strangers.

"Yes, it seems as if greed has overtaken my home as well," she replies. "But how do we rid the land of such a poison? How do we fight such a dark power?"

"On your journey, you will see that our power lies in numbers. You cannot destroy evil, only outnumber it. Greed and benevolence are like fire and water. Both equally powerful, the winner is only decided by the masses. Do the waves diffuse the flames, or do the flames consume the waters? There is power in numbers, Princess. My people have a saying: *I am because we are*. We are greater together.

"My people have that same saying," She stops and thinks for a moment, becoming lost in her own memories before continuing.

"I've lost everyone I love. I am alone here," A single tear drops from each eye as the princess hangs her head with heavy despair. I urge her to finish her tonic; she will need all the help she can get. Life in this realm can hold much sorrow, but for now there is no time for tears, so I go on.

"You will find that the very thing that opposes you will push you to the greatest heights of yourself if you are strong, and the very depths of yourself if you are weak. These are all things to consider, Princess, because the journey you have been given is a dangerous one. You must sow the seeds."

"How is it that you know these things?" she asks sharply. No doubt the realization of what must happen next is starting to reside within her, stirring her anger and raising her eternal fire.

"My ancestors are what my people call spirit guides. They guide me from the Earth. My ancestors knew yours. They were explorers who traded with us. Our people shared knowledge and stories that advanced our magic on both sides. I was born to fulfill a mission. My mission in this realm is to restore the connection of all of us Earth children, descendants of the first children of God. We are all different by design. Sky Mother made us that way so we would learn to share, and not take.

People of Eastern, Western, Northern and Southern lands, all connected under one sky. The wind directs all our paths, the trees provide us all with nourishment, and our dreams instruct us. I honor those signs, and in return I live in peace and abundance as an important part of Sky Mother's plan. And when my mission is complete, I will rejoin with my family."

"Where is your family?" she asks softly, as if she already knows the answer.

I take a deep breath and reply "when the Europeans came, they . enslaved us first. Slavery with us Natives only lasted for a little while. Disease ran rampant and wiped out many. Our women were defiled, and our homes were taken from us. We were forced to travel across to lands unknown. A lot of us natives banded together against the Europeans, even though many of our own assimilated and fought alongside the Europeans against us. In order to survive, my family banded with other tribes who were allies to us. They were familiar with the middle and northern lands. They are now living on the crooked river in the northern Cuyahoga valley. The Cuyahoga valley is lush. There are three tribes living there now along with some escaped Africans that made the journey with them. They canoe along the river and hunt on the shores. Some tribes choose to live closer to the lake that surrounds the river. Near the lake named Erie, there is often stormy weather. The water quickly gets whipped up by winds. The Native tribes and the Africans are safe there. They live in isolation because of the terrain. When I fulfill my purpose, I will join them. Through it all, we continue to worship God, our ancestors and the spirits living and once living. That is how I stay connected to my family when I am far from them.

"Yes...yes, I believe my ancestors guide me as well, even here- in this *place*. Thank you for the tonic. Is it, sassafras... and mint?"

"Sassafras, mint and mullein, to protect you and empower you."

"Thank you. I will need all my strength. I leave to find my people tonight."

"You must first rest. Then we leave."

"I will first prepare a table and wait for my ancestors to meet me there. They will instruct me."

I nod in agreement. We finish our tonic before preparing a small table. On it, we place a few wildflowers that grow here in the woods. Lesedi carefully places the purple lotus in the center. Around it, we leave some bread with honey, a clay bowl with fresh water, a jade stone, and a feather. I instruct Lesedi to stay in the tent. I will secure our meal while she prays for guidance. She will need it for the trip ahead.

# CHAPTER 8 *LESEDI*

I sit on my knees and bow my head to pray. Instantly, I am back flying through the black abyss. When I land, I am at our sacred center back in Elegua. I hear water. It rushes from the center; clear and fresh as it floods my feet. It is cool and refreshing to the touch. The water beneath my bare feet circles and forms together to form a long slender body with long locs of water. *Mama.* Dressed in the cool blue of the river›s waves and wearing seven silver bracelets. A single shell around her neck. Mama has become one with the water.

"Mama!" I cry. Seeing her triggers a rush of emotion that I cannot contain. "Please, take me home," I try to continue frantically, but the words don't come fast enough and are replaced with tears.

"My darling girl, don›t hold your tears; let them flow, let them heal you, and let them give you strength. You›re going to need your mind to be clear. There is a long road ahead of you. My baby girl, you are a woman now, and you must be ready to listen to what your heart tells you to do."

Like a brokenhearted child with tear-filled eyes, I wipe them with both hands and look up at my Mama. "I think it›s saying, find Baba and find Kendi and come up with a plan to get us home."

"Then that is what you must do, and you must not deny anyone who seeks you for refuge. There are many who have lost their homes and families. You must carry all who come to you."

"How will I do that Mama? I don›t know the land, all I have is the seeds hiding in my hair. I have no time to sow them. How will we eat? How will we make the journey? How will we defend ourselves?"

"Are you not trained in the ways of the staff as well as the ways of the land? Are you not of magical descent? Are you not the chief?" Mama says with finality.

"This land is very similar to the land that made us. The gatekeeper that you encountered in the woods will guide you. His tribe has lived in this land for many generations. Follow the path, you don›t need to know everything now. Let the path reveal itself to you as you move in your purpose. Your first task is to find your Baba and restore his magic. My healing, dreaming queen of Elegua, this is your moment. Do what you do best, heal and dream."

I think about Mama's words for a moment. "Restore the magic? But how?" Mama answers my unspoken question.

"If you boil a petal of the sacred lotus, it will create a tonic that restores the magic of whoever consumes it. One petal is more than enough. But I must warn you, Lesedi, be very selective of who you choose to restore. When the last pedal is gone, the lotus will be forever lost. A power so strong, such as the lotus' is easy to abuse. Be sure the drinker of the tonic is a worthy bearer of the most precious gift.

Mama's words wash over me. So much to take in. She is right of course, but am I ready for this? Maybe the ancestors made a mistake. *Or maybe I was chosen.* I am snatched back to the other alternate reality happening right now with Mama. With gentle eyes, she looks at me and says "Ask the gatekeeper of his knowledge of captors in this area. I am sure where the captors reside, our enslaved loved ones are close by. You cannot do this alone, Lesedi. You must find your own tribe here, create a family for yourself and use the power of the many to help you carry the heavy load."

My chest feels as if it could explode any moment. I'm overwhelmed with stress and worry, but also, I feel a sense of pride and new strength. It is almost as if I have always trained for this and did not know. For the first time I will have to assert all my knowledge. What I've learned of the trees and plants, my knowledge of the staff, all has led me to this moment. I will let all six of my senses lead me. I know of protection and of violence. *And I know of magic.* I smiled, a real smile for the first time since I left my village. Behind my smile I taste the bitterness of revenge on my tongue.

"My daughter, there is nothing that you are not capable of. You have power. Use it the way Sky Mother intended: for the good of us all."

And with that, Mama was gone. I fell into a black abyss. In the blink of an eye, everything that was once in front of me is gone, and I am back in the woods with the gatekeeper.

"Chief Running Bull, do you know of any places nearby where captors reside with enslaved Africans?"

"Yes, of course. I know of many. There are two just some miles down the road. It's about half a day's walk away. The first captor is of French descent. He refers to himself as the benevolent one. He claims his slaves are happy and well taken care of. He is gluttonous and lives a life of excess."

The second is the plantation of an evil man who calls himself a slave breaker. He came here from another place in the Southeast lands looking to make his money in Louisiana. He says he's known where he comes from for turning Africans into obedient slaves. "

"Will you show me the way?"

"I do not leave these woods, but I will tell you the way. And I will meet you when the task is complete."

Slowly and deliberately, Chief Running Bull begins to explain the landscape to me. He talks of Magnolia trees, oak trees, and a swamp covered in Spanish moss. He says, "look for them and follow them." The land will lead me. When I get to a break in the ground that is called a levy, I know I am close. I must cross the swamp, being sure to protect myself from the mosquitos and gators. In front of the swamp lay the slave quarters built behind this "benevolent" master's plantation. I will start there in search of my family.

Before I start on my journey, I wander the woods for a while to see what plants I can find. The woods are abundant with the things I will need to carry with me. I pick as much as I can carry in an animal skin satchel given to me by the gatekeeper. With the seeds I carried through the middle passage in my hair and my purple Lotus close to my scalp, I secured them for the last time and began to braid long intricate braids, pulling them up in a tight circular bun to ensure their safety. Chief Running Bull says the journey will take half of a day, so I will leave at twilight.

That night, the wind blows in only one direction with conviction, leading me down a straight path towards my destiny. The aisle of trees in front of me bustles from the force of the aerial pathway the night breeze commanded. Dark tree trunks shine in shadows illuminated by the moon. Above, the silhouettes of their fruits loom. The sounds of chirps and howls rule the night. Despite the threat the dark brings about, I am in a state of tranquility. The trees serve as my protection. I stay close to them. I feel them steady me as I prepare me for the peril that awaits me.

Further down my dark illuminated path, I reach the bayou behind the slave quarters. The sky is a purplish shade of pink, and I know the morning sun is near. The bayou echoes with the sounds of frogs croaking, cicadas humming, and mosquitoes buzzing. It looks a lot like the small swamps and rivers around the village back home. It is unsettling how similar this new land is to Elegua. It has the same red clay dirt roads, and the same lush green bushes. It is almost like a cruel trick to be so far away from home, and yet still feel so close to it.

Swamps are not for the weak. Like all water, they are sacred and powerful. If you are not equipped for their power, they will consume you. But the swamp holds more than just death. It serves a dual purpose: the opaque waters hold the innate power to both decompose and restore. Despite its suffocating and murky contents, plant and animal life flourish here. The swamp is the life cycle. Just like in Elegua, life starts in the dark dampness of the mud, bringing back into existence what was lost to the darkness.

A walk through the swamp will not be a fast or easy one. You must wade the decomposing waters. I make sure to carry with me the right herbs to protect against insects and leeches. I keep the small leather satchel in my bosom to protect it. Before I step in, I take a long glance over the surface, watching for waves that may be signs of gators lurking nearby. I take slow and deliberate steps, intricately moving through the living and nonliving creatures inhabiting the mud beneath my feet. Hours seem like days as the morning sun begins to rise. It is already intense in its heat. Each step gets heavier and heavier. All my senses are buzzing, and I realize in the pit of my stomach is the feeling of unease. I feel as though I'm being watched. The willow trees and hanging moss covered branches surrounding the swamp are dressed in fog, making it impossible to see what or *who* may be lurking among them. I can't afford to stop to get a closer look, so I keep moving. I increase my pace as anxiety starts to set in. My heart is pounding like war drums and sweat drips in my eyes. The long sleeves of the fabric dress given to me by the Gatekeeper protects me from the buzzing mosquitoes, but they slow me down. The deep brown water has made my white long-sleeve dress a shade of deep brown to match my deep brown skin. I can only hope that I blend in with the swamp, making me invisible to whatever or whoever is watching through the fog. When I finally make it to the shore, I wobble out of the water in exhaustion. Still feeling as if I can feel eyes watching me, I know I can't stay here long. My legs beg me to rest but I power on, making sure to stay as hidden as possible.

In the distance, I can see small wooden huts behind a massive white building. I know I've reached the slave quarters. Then suddenly, the sounds of bells echo all around me. I run to the nearest bush and duck down low. From here I have a view. At the sound of the bells, brown bodies begin emerging from the quarters. I made it. What awaits me now scares me more than ever.

# CHAPTER 9 *ESTHER*

Lord let me get on up and start this day before my baby get to fussin'. I know those bells gone be ringing any minute now. Another day, I›m thankful the Lord gave me life, but another day I must live as a slave on this godforsaken plantation. The birds are chirping, the chickens are clucking, and the sun is up, which means it›s time to get to work. I can't oversleep again. I know James is going to start to wonder why soon. I haven›t got the heart to tell him. Instead, I pull myself out of bed and nurse my baby. I slice a few pieces of bread for James and me with some peach jam I jarred myself spread over it. On the side, I add a few pieces of dried ham, then I wake James for breakfast. Every morning I shake his big bear shoulders. He smiles before he opens his eyes. A big white smile on a big black man.

"Come on and get up James, ain't got time for sleep."

"Good morning, wife," he replies with a wide grin. I smiled back. Our love is deep and true. I pray for the day we can be free to live together without the constant threat that is always hanging over us. James gets up and takes Lilly from my arms. He tickles her while making silly sounds. The sight warms my heart. We all laugh for a moment until we are interrupted by the sound of a rooster singing its morning song. Laughter stops and reality starts to set in again. James and I have a silent meal together with Lilly. We share a brief kiss, before I wrap my hair and strap the baby to my back. James grabs his machete, and we head out to the sounds of the bells.

Outside, work has already begun. On my way to the fields, I do my daily check of the plantation. I check to make sure everything I know of the layout here is still intact. My eyes know exactly what to look for, knowing instantly if anything is out of place. I know every tree and every rock. The map of the land is always painted clearly in my head. Every open space and every blind spot. I'd been planning my escape for as long as I can remember. The landscape has become my daily mantra.

My eyes scan the familiar features trying to make out what this unfamiliar thing was I was looking at. Hiding in the bushes is a dirty brown woman slave huddled with her knees to her chest. My heart starts to pound. She is no doubt a runaway slave looking for someone. That's the only reason she'd come this close to a plantation while on the run. I immediately start off back towards the slave quarters. I must get to her discreetly and quickly. My heart drops as I see overseer Wayne peer from behind the barn. He's found her. I stop and try to look busy. Lucy is passing by, carrying a basket on her head and two in her arms of laundry. I offer to assist her, and she happily hands me a basket. When we hear the shrill voice crack, we watch with the familiar feeling of impending doom as Wayne gives vision of his dirty tobacco-stained teeth.

"Well, well look what we got here. Looks like we done found us a runaway. She fell right into our laps, now what are the odds of that. What's your name girl and who's your master?" he says, yanking her by her dirty dress. The woman has a determined look on her face and refuses to answer. When his questions go unanswered a second time, he smacks her to the ground. "I'm going to show you how we deal with runaways around here."

We all look on with horror as he drags her to a tree stomp and hogties her hands around them. Wayne then goes into the barn nearby. When he returns, he's carrying a bullwhip. He whips her hands, arms, back, and legs. Blood began to mix with the mud stained in her dirty dress. She sits still. Face scowled, mouth twisted and unmoved.

After the beating overseer Wayne left her there and told no one to bother her or we'd be next. She lay exhausted on the stoop, sweating, bleeding and dirty.

The air is thick with the summer's heat. It's another day of grueling backbreaking work. The distraction of the mystery woman keeps my mind occupied. When the master finally comes that afternoon with his black mistress on his arm, Wayne informs him proudly of his discovery.

"Hmm," master replies as he eyes her seriously with a tobacco pipe hanging out of his mouth. Finally, he turns to Zoya and asks, "What do you think, my dear? Should we dispose of her, or should we keep her?"

The beautiful dark woman replies "My dear, let her know of your kindness. Maybe her rebellious soul will be subdued by your benevolence."

"My dear, you are right," He says as he kisses her on the cheek. He then turns to Wayne and says "untie this girl and see that the women see to her. She'll join them tomorrow with their chores." And with that, John is summoned. John arrives with Jake and carefully they carry her to the empty cottage at the end of the slave quarters.

The slave quarters are buzzing with the news of the found runaway slave woman. Everybody is wondering where she came from and who she's looking for. That evening, the women gather greens, rice, tomatoes, and okra for Julie to make a stew. James sometimes helps Luke in the blacksmith shop. At my request, James is able to get a couple spoons. I grab some clay bowls from a shelf in our cabin. Nanny directs the children as they help collect buckets of water that would be boiled and returned to the buckets. Sable goes to her cabin and grabs a simple clean dress from an old oak chest. Moments later Anna comes out of her cabin at the same time as her neighbor Lucy, one hand holding an old sheet, and the other an old quilt.

"Wait!" Running up the road from the big house is Rachell. Her wild red curls and olive toned face make her look like a wild cat.

"I only just heard about the woman. If yalls going to see about her, I'd like to come."

"You got here just in time then," I say, handing her the utensils with a smile. I grab the other side of Julie's heavy pot and she sighs with relief. All together we women set out to the abandoned cabin.

When we enter the cabin, we find the woman half asleep, sweating and shaking. Nanny walks over to her and puts the back of her hand to the woman's forehead.

"She needs water," Nanny says without breaking contact with the woman. Rachell dips a bowl into the last bucket and brings it over to Nanny. Slowly, she tips the bowl into her mouth, not spilling a drop. The woman sleepily opens her eyes and starts speaking what I know to be the mother tongue.

"It sounds like she is speaking the same language as that other new slave," Rachell says seriously. "Might be a good idea to go fetch him later." We all nod in agreement.

"I wonder if that's who she›s looking for," Julie says in a soft reply. "We couldn't understand him when he tried to tell us his name."

"We can't understand you dear," Nanny is saying warmly to the woman. "But if you can understand me, please know us women here ain't gone hurt ya. You can trust us."

The bond we all share is unspoken and strong. Our vow to protect one another is deeply rooted. She reaches out weakly and takes Nanny's hand and gives it a small squeeze. Nanny tops her hand with her own and says, "There, there child."

Nanny and Anna sit her up. With us, we brought three hot buckets of water and one cool for drinking. Julie pulls some rags from the kitchen out from her apron. Rachell mimics the motion, also reaching in her apron. We circle around the bed and begin to clean the woman. Sable starts humming a quiet song of sorrow and strength. We all join in with her as we perform the task. Delicately, each woman takes turns taking rags to the buckets after wiping the blood and thick layers of dirt from her dark skin and hair. Humming and diligently working, we wash all the dirt away, carefully, and softly dabbing her wounds. When three buckets are brown as swamp water, we remove the dirty fabrics and replace it with a clean dress. We cover and dress each wound with clean rags. When the task is done, we gently lift her and place beneath her the sheet. Delicately returning her to the bed, we cover her with the quilt. Julie then softly speaks over her, "Miss if you can hear me, I'm going to try to feed you some soup now. Don't be alarmed," and she slowly and gently places the spoon of warm stew in her mouth. The woman looks right away as if the stew is helping to restore the color to her face. Her eyes open and close again with delight as she swallows the warm spoonful. Through a small strained but heavy accented voice the woman whispered "stew," Julie who has been looking on with wide sympathetic eyes hastily moves closer to the bed again with a chuckle and speaks. "See I told yall, my stew can heal anything," We all let out a little laugh and groaned. We know Julie is right and she never lets us forget it.

After a short contemplation I say to the group "I'll stay here tonight and see to it Wayne or his sons don't make themselves comfortable in her presence while she lay ill. Master will expect her to work tomorrow, no doubt."

"That's good thinking, Esther," Lucy says.

"We'll let James know when we head back," Nanny adds.

"Just leave that extra stew for me and I'll be just fine here," We exchange hugs and gather up what needed to be taken out with the women returning to their cabins. After emptying the dirty water out back, there is one bucket left with clean water to wash myself up a little. I then start a fire and decide to look around. Franny has left behind a lot of bottles and jars with half-filled contents and a few drying herbs. None of us knows what she used it for. Over the fire, I place a kettle, deciding I will have tea ready if the now sleeping mystery slave awakens. When I turn around from the fire, I jump back startled by the once sleeping woman who is now sitting straight up and staring at me.

"I'm sorry," she says in her heavy accented voice. "I didn›t mean to scare you. I noticed there was peppermint and sage growing there in those pots," and she pointed across the room to a slave made pot in the windowsill.

"Can you add a few leaves to the kettle for tea, please?"

"Yes of course," I hurry over to the window, my mind now buzzing again. She has been ill and sleeping, but somehow, she saw that. How did she see that, and how does she know that? Is she a medicine woman? Does she know land? If so, how'd she get herself caught up here? Just then, the door to the cabin opens. In the doorway is my James with my Lilly tied to his back with one of my clothes.

"I just came to make sure you were alright. Nanny told me you would be staying here tonight."

"Yes, I hope you don't mind. It's just she's new here, and she's ill and I don't want her to have to wake up alone."

"You're a good woman, Esther," he says with a smile and gives me a kiss to my forehead." I brought this for you, and out of the fabrics that held Lilly, James' bear hand removes a small bible. With a small grin and a small shushing gesture of one finger to his lip, he extends it to me. I quickly grab the bible and place it in my apron. I wrap my arms around my strong man that I love dearly and give him one more knowing look before he sets back out into the night. When I close the cabin door, I go back to pouring tea for me and the woman.

"What is your name?" she asks.

"Esther. What's yours?"

"Lesedi"

"It's a pleasure to meet you, Lesedi. Let's have some tea shall we," I say, handing her a dented tin mug.

"Was that your husband and baby?"

"Yes, my husband James and my baby girl Lilly."

"She's beautiful."

"Thank you. Do you have any youngins?"

"No. And thank the skies not. They'd probably be lost to me now just like the rest of my family." The pain and anger in her voice is clear through the heavy accent.

"Is that what brought you here? Looking for your family?"

"Yes. They were stolen from me. We were all stolen. I›m trying to find the people I love. I believe they are all here, and I will not stop until I find them."

The serious tone in her voice makes me wonder what this woman may be capable of. She had endured her punishment without a sound. And here she is now but hours later recovering and speaking of things that are unthinkable for a slave. Is she naïve or brave? As a child I mentioned, running away once over dinner around the fire in the slave quarters. Before I could think I was slapped by an older woman near me named Ophelia. She said I should know better than to voice such silly happenings out loud unless I was looking to be sold. That day, much like the day master sold my Mama will forever haunt me.

"Well, I will help you find your family as much as I can, but the master is strict about slaves not running away so we›ll have to be careful in how we find them."

"I'm thankful to have met you, Esther," She smiles my way. I return her smile. I feel thankful to have met her too, although I'm not sure why yet.

"Esther, can I ask something of you?"

"Yes, sure, anything."

"Can you tell me everything that I might need to know about this place?

"If anybody can tell you about this place, it's me. I've been here my whole life." I take a sip of tea and continue on. "Well, the most important thing to remember is to do your work and keep your head down. Don't speak unless you›re spoken to."

She nods as if to say she understands so I go on.

"The day starts when the bells ring. The women with children too small to work in the field will go with Nanny for the day. Nanny is too old to work now, but she's been on this plantation her whole life. Nanny raised the master. She was a servant to his mother. The master's mother loved Nanny dearly they say. She taught Nanny to read in secret. Only I know that. Nanny secretly taught me to read too after Master sold my mama. If it wasn't for Nanny taking me in, I would have been at the mercy of Wayne and his band just like the rest of the women."

Lesedi didn't say anything. She continued to listen with knowing eyes. "You should know the daily routine," I say, refilling our cups with tea. "Every morning Master wakes up after work has already begun. He takes his coffee, toast, and tobacco pipe on the front porch and meets with his slave driver-a slave man named John to plan the day's work. John is the only slave that Master trusts. We work together to conceal that John's loyalty is to the slaves. After giving his directions of what is to be done for the day, Master walks the grounds with his slave mistress, Zoya. It's a good thing the Mrs. is dead, she's probably rolling in her grave knowing a negro woman has taken her place as mistress over this here plantation."

"What do we grow here?" she asks curiously.

"Cotton originally, but mostly sugarcane now. The master's house stands on the road by the river. Behind the house are the fields and the road leading back to the sugar house near the slave quarters. Master owns all the land between the swamp and the river. Our cabins are about a half mile down the road behind the big house. The road goes through the center of the cabins and leads down to the sugar mill in front of the swamp. The big house was built by slaves so its craftsmanship is unmatched. It's a huge white house with a grand porch and tall pillars raised up by cypress and brick with secret hiding places all throughout it that the masters don't know about. Only the slaves know because they built it. The slave quarters were also built by slaves. The old master gave the slaves scraps to build with, and just like always, those slave men made magic out of it. Each family got a custom-made cabin, complete with loose boards and sliding bricks that concealed secret hiding places, and hidden compartments. No two cabins have the same hiding places."

"Hmmm," She says. "I wonder what secrets lie in this cabin. It was no doubt the home of a medicine woman."

"Are you a medicine woman?"

"An apprentice of sorts, I guess you could say," She replies with a smile. Her brown glowing eyes hold a look of pride, and sorrow.

"Master's gone be glad to know that. This cabin used to be a root woman named Franny's, but she ran away some time ago. Since then, we've been having to go down to the quarter to see Miss DuPont for help anytime there's sickness around. Master don't like us going around Miss DuPont because he don't want us to get the idea we could be free like her. So now we can only go when the illness is serious. Master doesn't want any more slaves to die. He says it's a waste of his hard-earned money." At the mention of the word free Lesedi's glowing eyes looked as if they had gotten brighter.

"Who is Miss DuPont?" she asked seriously.

"Monique DuPont is a free colored woman living down in the French Quarter. They say Monique's Mama was an African queen who was captured and sold into slavery. When her master saw her on the block, he was so taken with her beauty, he bought only her that day. As you could guess not long after the Queen gave birth to a child. A baby girl she named Monique. But not long after Monique was born, the master mysteriously died. In his last will and testament his family was shocked and horrified to discover that he had not only freed them but also left the queen and her daughter a large sum and a house down in the quarter, declaring them forever free. His wife claims the queen was a witch and she killed the master, but she could never prove it. The doctor said he died of a heart attack from years of overindulging in moon shine and ungodly women."

We both let out a laugh. We continue to talk like old friends that have been finally reunited. She tells of her homeland and her family, and a handsome man named Ukize who was her intended husband back home.

"Do you think I could stay here in this cabin, and take up the position as the healer here?"

"I don't see why not. I'll have Rachell mention it to Zoya. Rachell was just her with us. Zoya, the master's mistress, is her mother."

"And so that would mean..."
"Yes, the master is her father. Rachell works in the house, but her brother Ben works out in the fields and the sugar house. He tried to run once. Master sent the dogs on him and beat him bloody black and blue. The only reason he wasn't sold is because of Zoya. But ever since then Master goes out of his way to make life as hard for Ben as he can."

"His own son?"

"He's still a slave," The silence slowly crept in. The reality that we are not our own reignites my constant eternal flame.

"The slave quarters are the only place where we have a little control over our lives," I say in an attempt to change the mood. Our homes are small 2-bedroom brick and cypress cabins with a fireplace and a small cut out pantry. Each cabin holds an entire family. Slave women without a husband get matched to one by Master and made to bear his seed. It's Master's way of making sure he'll always have slaves. Each cabin has a bed, a table, and chairs. We cover the beds with quilts sewn by the women. Sable oversees all the sewing along with Lucy. Hanging over each fireplace are iron pots, pans and utensils made by the slave men in the blacksmith shop. We only cook inside in the cool months. During the summer we cook outside, and all eat together around the fire. Master lets us keep our own garden and raise our own livestock. Outside each cabin are views of rainbow-colored fruits and vegetables all in a row. Our garden is a magical place. A lot of the slave women brought seeds over from Africa in their hair. Those seeds are planted out behind our cabins. It's our little piece of the Motherland they got to bring with them."

"That sounds magical. I would love to see that."

"It's right out back. We don't work on Sundays so after church we can spend some time out there if you would like."

"And everyone is happy here? No one runs or fights back?"

"We pretend to be happy for our own livelihood. A lot of slaves who came here from other plantations do find pleasure in having the chance to make a few decisions for themselves, but how happy can one be when they are ripped away from their families? It is true that we do have a few more luxuries than say the slaves down the way at Robert Jackson's plantation. Where our master is greedy and careless, theirs is greedier and very careful. But where can you run when you do not know the land? All we have here is each other, and that is what we fight to protect. The right to have one another."

# CHAPTER 10 *LESEDI*

Over the next few days, I settled into my new home in the root woman's abandoned cabin. As I healed, I became clearer in what my purpose would be during my time spent here on the sugarcane plantation. Amid such a dark time, I felt encased by music, love, and warmth. I had no strength to say it that night, but I prayed in my head that Sky Mother would make the women I met aware of how grateful I was for their love and tender care. They did not know or ask to know me. They simply saw that I needed help and came to my aid. They rubbed oil on my wounds and wrapped them with bandages. After I was cleaned and dressed, one woman sat beside me and held me up while another spoon fed me some of the most delicious stew I had ever tasted. My belongings were neatly placed beside me, and I was covered with a quilt that felt as if it was the very same quilt home on my bed in Elegua. It warmed me from the inside out.

I vowed to do the same for them as long as I am here.

In order to accomplish my great task, I will need to learn as much about the people and the land as possible. I find that even here where talking isn›t allowed, the whispers hold a wealth of knowledge and information. With Africans working in the house, the fields and on the roads traveling to other plantations and into the quarters, there's a constant opportunity to exchange information and stories. I have learned that there are many plantations on the road that I now live on. They all line the river on a road that stretches for miles. I start to slowly plot my escape to the next plantation. Before I am ready, I will have to gather enough information and find my clan of future lotus bearers.

I›ve taken the position as the plantation's new medicine woman. I assist in the kitchen and fields as well. I spent the first few days picking herbs on the land and hearing about all the sickness and sores that have been going overlooked for so long. Without a proper healer, and with the master's fear of the mysterious Miss DuPont, simple illnesses have festered, and in some cases been fatal. The master made it clear to me I was to save as many slaves as possible. Every slave lost was money lost.

One morning as I am picking herbs, two men come running straight towards me. Sweating and out of breath, the tall and slender one asks "Are you the healer woman?"

"Yes, I am."

"There's a man you gotta see about right now."

"If you all can carry him, bring down to the old cabin at the end. I'll go get ready," The men then run back towards the field. I run back to the cabin and start boiling water. I've been sleeping in the second room of the cabin to keep the front empty and available for moments such as this. Thinking back to my Mama Oni's cabin, I start to visualize the hanging herbs and their various uses as called out by my healing grandmother. I look in the stores of herbs that I have gathered and anticipated the men's return.

A few minutes later, four men enter carrying a long and strongly built dark black man.

"Lay him down on that bed there. What happened?" A not so tall man with chiseled features, golden yellow skin, wavy black hair, and bright brown eyes was staring at me so intensely as he answered.

"Don't know, miss. We were all working chopping down the cane when he dropped. We think he passed out from the heat. But he landed on his machete. He's not accustomed to it yet, you see, he's new here."

For a second, I find myself distracted by the deepness in the man's eyes. As my brain remains in a brief fog, my body takes over to do the work I knew had to be done. My feet move on their own accord. As I move in to get a closer look, I cannot believe what or better yet *who* was before my eyes. The yam farmer lies there bloody and breathing heavy. The trader. Had it not been for him, my family would still be together in our village. I felt the heat rise in my chest. A cloud of red distorts all my senses. My anger boils and spills over. Before I can stop myself, I am yelling at the top of my lungs in my mother tongue, having every intention of making it known to the farmer who I am.

"YOU! TREACHEROUS TRADER! OH, HOW SWEET THE SKIES ARE TO HAVE DELIVERED YOU TO THE SAME FATE!"

At the sound of my foreign yells of anger, three of the four men who carried in the trader looked at each other and ran out. The golden man remains alone with eyes wide as he watches me. The bleeding yam farmer's eyes open as wide as saucers upon hearing the native language and seeing my angry Eleguan face.

Too weak to respond, his eyes reclosed. A look of hopelessness rests on his face.

Just then, Wayne bursts through the door unannounced and without knocking. He first looks at the golden skinned man and says "ain't you got work to do, boy. That cane ain't gone chop itself, or should I tell daddy you out here tryna escape again?"

The man scowls, the veins in his neck and arm bulging. He then turns to me and says, "the name is Ben, if you need any further assistance send for me," before turning around and walking out the cabin.

"Is he dead?" Wayne asks me plainly.

"No, he is not. I should have him patched up in no time."

"Well hurry up gal time is money. I expect to see him back in the fields tomorrow."

"But it may be infected. It'll be at least a few days until he can work again."

The overseer is now walking closer to me. I could see his brown teeth and smell his foul odor.

"Are you sassing me gal, because I don't take kindly to slaves telling me what they gone do. If he's not out on the field in the morning, I expect to see you out there in his place."

Feeling my anger return to me, I try to keep it under wraps, but the rebel in me cannot. Or will not.

"This is infected, and I don't have what I need. Master is not going to be happy about losing another slave. They've been dropping like flies around here lately from what the master has been saying."

Wayne's eyes burn. Before he can respond, the doorway is again occupied without invitation. Master walks in ahead of Zoya, who has her nose in a bouquet of what looks like freshly pulled flowers. When she lifts her head and takes one look at the man on the bed. she freezes in her place, her face a pale shade.

Master takes no notice of Zoya's stunned appearance. Instead, he walks to me and asks, "Will he live?"

"Maybe, sir. The wound is infected, you see. I need some things to get rid of the fever, but I don't see them here. If I could get those few things, I could make a salve for the infection and stitch it back up. I think I saw some stitching materials left around here somewhere."

Master thinks for a moment. His face is serious. No one speaks or moves in the wake.

"You will be permitted to take one trip to the quarter to see the negro healer miss Dupont. You are to retrieve all the supplies you will need and return. Your pass will be for 2 hours. Rachell will accompany you to ensure you find your way back. We wouldn't want any mishaps now would we now."

"No sir."

"Then it›s settled. Zoya my darling, upon our return let Rachell know of her task."

It appears hearing the master call her name awakened her from the trance placed on her by the traitorous farmer.

"Yes, dear." She replies blankly.

And they all step out of the door and start on their trek back to the big house. Wayne looks back with a menacing grin and a tip of his dirty straw hat.

My attention now returns to the farmer. I walk up closely to the bed to get a good look at him. Then I begin to clean his wound with the boiling water. I take no care for his wincing at the sting of the heat.

The farmer says in a low voice "You would be justified to let me die. I know the nature of your people would compel you to save me instead, but it is my preference not to live."

"I will not reward you with the luxury of death," I snapped.

"Ahhh," he winces. "And here I was praying that you would. Sky mother is vengeful indeed. "

"Don't you dare blame the skies! Your greed and your betrayal led us here, nothing more."

"Perhaps you are right. Go from me now. Let me die in peace."

"I vow to keep you alive, if for nothing more so you'll be constantly reminded of your treachery."

I work in silence on the weak man. It is true, the work in the fields and the strain have taken its effect on the man. I am wrapping his wounds with hot cloth and herbs when a small soft tap raps on the door. Upon calling enter, Rachelle walks through the front door. Today, her wild red hair is wrapped tightly in cloth on top of her head.

She walks straight up to me and embraces me in a warm hug. "It's good to see you. How are you today, Miss D? I hope you don't mind us calling you that. A few of the folks here have a hard time with motherland names."

"No not at all," I smile back. "It's good to see you too, Rachell."

"I saw my brother Ben in passing, he said the two of you have met."

I think back to the brown eyes that studied me this morning and replied "Yes, he was very helpful."

"Good. This man here is named Mason. He's the one we were telling you about who also speaks your language. Maybe the two of you can talk a little when we return. Well come on let's get a move on. John is in the stable with the wagon. Master gave him a pass to drive us down to Miss Dupont's.''

The patient appears to now be sleeping. It is a little after midday and the perfect time to head down to the quarter before all the shops close for the day.

Together, Rachell and I head down the road towards John. John is a tall and strong man with muscles defined and brown skin the color of leaves changing in the fall. He appears to be a very serious man who doesn't smile or exchange pleasantries. His mind, heart, and soul seem to be guarded heavily.

When we approach the barn, John tips his hat but does not speak. Aware of the task at hand, he pockets his pass and helps us into the wagon. Along the dirt road, we see people riding on everything from horses, to donkeys, to cows into the crowded bustling quarters. Business is being conducted all around. People of every color moving with purpose. We approach what Rachelle calls Congo square before finally stopping at a small white house with a sign hanging in front of the raised porch that reads 'Monique's Medicine and Apothecary'.

The white steps look to have been swept with red brick dust. As we approach the door, smells of cinnamon and sage greet us first.

Rachelle knocks lightly on the door, and it creaks open. Slowly we walk through.

Inside the house is decorated beautifully. There is a parlor and a dining room, all adorned with candles, plants, and wooden figurines all over the house. Lavish pictures and paintings of people and abstracts hang on the wall. A brilliant chandelier sparkled from the center of the room and the walls are painted a sweet shade of pinkish purple. From out of the darkness steps a beautiful light brown skin woman dressed in a lavender purple dress. Her locced hair is wrapped in a matching lavender tignon. Up her arms are clashing golden bangles that shined like the sun. The craftsmanship of the gold is as fine as what we traded with the Akan's in the market back home.

The woman says in an accented voice. "Rachelle, it is so good to see you. I am shocked Andre has let his captives off the plantation. Who is dying?" She asks with a bit of amusement. She then stops and turns to me before warmly saying "I am Monique, and you are?"

"I am Lesedi," I replied. "It is a pleasure to meet you."

"Hmm Lesedi," she says as she contemplates my existence by eyeing me unmoving. "Are you a healer, Lesedi?" She asks as if she already knew the answer.

"Of sorts I guess you could say." I replied.

"Come sit with me, I know our time is limited. Rachell, if you don't mind, can you see to it that John gets a few apples for his stallion and some water I left out back. Lesedi and I will be just a moment. Follow me Lesedi," she says as she led me up a flight of stairs into her study. Inside, there are more plants, candles, figurines, a table and chairs, and a wide deck of cards.

"Please sit," she says gesturing to a chair at the table. Warm sunlight pours through the window, and frankincense burns nearby.

"Shall we see what is in the cards for you?" She begins shuffling the deck. Her long slim fingers move with speed and precision. "A three-card spread for today," she carefully flips the first card and says "Hmm, the high priestess, Miss Ida is coming through first. She says you have divine wisdom, a gift from your foremothers. Slow down and consult your felt sense and inner voice. Embrace the mysteries of life. Let the spirit guides lead you," She flips the second card. "Ahh, the ancestors are next. That is very telling. My dear, your journey will be long and plagued with much discomfort. You will learn along the way the only thing constant is change. Every end is a new beginning. The ace of baskets confirms this," she says, flipping the final card. "There is beauty in the struggle. A flower will bloom in a dark place. This is a theme you are familiar with, no?"

"Yes," I reply in a whisper. "Very much so."

"Yes. So now that that is out of the way, how can I help you? What brings you to me?"

"Well, I've taken the position of healer woman. There is a man with an infected wound, but the stores in my cabin are empty. I am here to purchase the necessary materials to keep the workers alive. Master says he's losing too many slaves. He's tasked me with making sure whoever falls ill makes a full recovery.

"I see. Tell me Lesedi, do you have the flower?"

My eyes widened. "How did you know...?" I stammer before my voice fades.

"That is neither here nor there. The man that lay ill in your care is not the man you think he is." She flips another card before saying "The son of coins. He is telling us the importance of utilizing all your resources, even those you may have deemed unworthy. You will need him to execute your plan. The cards are telling you, Lesedi, that you have all you need. My advice to you is that you take one pedal from the sacred lotus and brew it. It shall create a tonic that is enough to restore what has been lost. Invite your chosen for tea and drink with them. As your journey continues, remember to honor the ancestors. Pour libations into the earth for those we have lost and ancestors will open the way for you and ensure that no force deters you. I will send you home with a few items from my stores to please your master. John, I'm sure will handle the compensation as always." She moves across the room with grace before opening the doors to a wardrobe lined with shelves and removes a few items. On the table before me, she places a large glass vial with crushed dried roots and flowers inside. Beside it, she sets down a jar with dark dried berries.

"This is echinacea. Also known as the coneflower. It is a powerful healing flower. It can be used as a treatment for infection or as an offering. These are elderberries. You can consume them to boost your health, or you can add them to your bathing water to help you with removing dark energy. Take these with you and complete your task. I will see you next week," she says with a smile as we walk towards the door and down the stairs where Rachelle is waiting with John.

"Next week?" I ask curiously.

"Yes, next week," She replies with a happy smile. With that, we say our goodbyes and make our way back through Congo square as we head back to the sugarcane plantation.

# CHAPTER 11 *MASOZI*

I awakened to an empty cabin. The pain in my arm was better now, but I still felt sick to my stomach. My head was throbbing, and I was cold and sweating at the same time. If only I could have some water. I looked around and saw nothing but hanging plants and empty vials. I thought "surely this is how I will die." Just then, the door creaked, and a small crack of sunlight peeked through it. The door stayed ajar, but no one entered. I sat up to get a better look. Slowly, a hand pushed open the door. In walked a dark skinned tall and slim woman dressed in a brilliant shade of yellow. The master's mistress closed the door quietly and walked slowly across the room with her eyes glued to the floor. Her face was lined, and her hair was tinged with streaks of gray, but still her beauty held youth. I eyed her curiously as she made her way through the room. She did not speak, and her eyes would not meet mine. She walked over by the fireplace and stood there with her hands interlaced in front of her.

I looked up and said in the mother tongue, "The healer woman is not here. I don›t know where she is or when she will return."

I was sure she did not understand, but I only know a few words of this new language. Not enough to converse yet, but I understand enough to get by.

Without lifting her head or her eyes she meekly replied in broken mother tongue, "I am aware. That is why I›m here. Tell me, how is your Baba?"

I froze, Unable to move, unable to answer, and unable to breathe. All the pain seemed to have left me. I couldn't feel my body. I stood numb taking in her appearance fully. This woman, her face is my face.

"Mama?" My voice cracked like a child on the break of tears. She did not answer. Heavy tears were now streaming down her face. I sat in shock, unmoving. She quickly wiped her tears and regained her calmness. In a stronger voice now, she said "I just wanted to come here and see you for myself. I told Andre to buy you that day I saw you on the block. I knew it was you. You have my face, but your father's eyes." She looked at me for the first time. She was fighting hard to keep the emotion off her face. A futile effort.

"I just wanted you to know that I did not abandon you. That I would have never abandoned you. I was kidnapped, and I was brought here. I never thought I'd see you again."

Before I could respond the door swung open again. It was the Eleguan healer and the red-haired house servant.

"Hello, Mother," the red-haired girl said as she entered the small cabin and placed a kiss on her cheek. My eyes shot between all three women standing before me, my head dizzy with confusion. Mama turned to the Eleguan and asked if she had what she needed. She nodded yes. Mama then said "Good, I will report back to Andre that all is well." Without a second look back, she was gone.

Still in a daze from what just happened, I hardly noticed the angry Eleguan woman staring at me with her hands on her hips. She was too young to look so much like someone's angry grandmother about to dish out some discipline.

"Yes?" I asked her sarcastically. Her eyes got smaller, now looking even more like an angry old lady.

"I am just trying to decide if I should let you suffer more for your smugness. Luckily for you, the ancestors told me to have pity on your soul. If I were you, I'd pray right now a prayer of gratitude!" she snapped. She was moving around the cabin now, readying random things. Red-hair sat in a chair nearby watching the interaction. I could not help but laugh a little. I don't know why. This woman, although powerful, I knew she was an Eleguan, seemed harmless. The more she threatened me, the more the goodness of her shined through. However, my little chuckle seemed to have angered her because just then she stormed over to me. Before I knew what was happening, I realized I'd been slapped. And hard. My arm instantly flew to my face, and I winced again, forgetting the pain in my arm that had now returned with a vengeance. In our native language she said. "Don't laugh at me you jackal."

She didn't look so innocent after that. But then it dawned on me, like a tidal wave. The seriousness of what I'd done. How I changed the course of our history and our home with one decision. How a life of misery, and an act of greed can affect an entire generation and their descendants. It was clear to me now, why the Eleguans lived so modestly, and why they chose to give rather than receive. That was the source of their wealth. Their values, their family, their traditions, all brought them wealth. It was clear this was our home now. And although I have accepted my fate as one who is forever doomed, the Eleguan princess has not, or will not believe the same. Her fire still burns. My fire died out long ago but maybe, if I can assist her, I can shift my fate.

When she saw me wince, I saw the concern in her face. Handing me a tin cup she said "here, drink this." While I drank, she slowly went to work on my wounded arm. I felt warm hot rags, as she cleaned the infected area. The water she used had fresh herbs boiling in its steamy vapors. The smell opened up all my senses, and the tea she handed me warmed me from the inside out.

My old bandages were replaced with new ones. I felt relaxed and easy. I asked her calmly "what is this I'm drinking?"

"Coneflower," she replied.

"Thank you," I said sincerely. She stopped and looked at me with an unreadable look before replying. "You're welcome."

Red-Hair, who I assume stayed to make sure the princess was okay, now had decided the situation was controlled enough for her to return to her chores in the house. Before she left, I heard the Eleguan address her as Rachell. She asked her if she could get a message to Esther. Rachell replied "Yes of course, Ms. D. See you tonight" before exiting.

The cabin was quiet once again. Neither of us spoke. Finally, she turned to me and said, "Why did you do it?" Her eyes were sad. I spoke honestly and replied "For a chance at what I thought was a better life. I've been struggling all my life for no fault of my own. I was just a product of my parent's sins, or so I thought. I grew up believing my mother abandoned our family because my Baba had an issue with too much palm wine. I had to be the man of the house as a child. I did the farming and the bartering. I kept money hidden so my Baba didn't squander it. Many days I had to wake him up and drag him inside because he lay in a deep wine induced sleep underneath the trees. When the outsider came and offered me the chance to leave it all behind, I thought sacrificing everyone else would be worth it. In my eyes you all had lived a privileged life and had no idea the poverty that was forced upon me. I thought it was only fair that the tables be turned. I realized today how ignorant I've been."

I went on to tell her about how the mistress came to tell me her true identity, and how she didn't abandon us. Her fate was the same as ours was now. And I now remembered that my poor Baba took to palm drinking in her absence only to cure his broken heart, not before.

When I was done, she did not speak. She only looked at me with those same unreadable eyes. Finally, she said "I guess we should eat. I'm going to go grab a few things from the garden. There's a fresh tin of water there if you need it." And with that she was out the door. I breathed a sigh of relief feeling much lighter now that I laid down my burden. It further cemented my decision to aid the princess in whatever plan was churning in her head. She was an Eleguan after all. The people here may not know their power, but I'd seen it first-hand. And I was willing to bet the skies that soon they would too.

# CHAPTER 12 *LESEDI*

It was just before dusk. The sky was decorated in brilliant shades of pink, orange, and purple as the sun got ready to set for the day. The enslaved workers were returning to the quarters from their various jobs around the plantation. Outback by the garden, a huge fire was lit in preparation for tonight's dinner. It was a beautiful summer night, so most of the workers and their children would undoubtedly eat outside together. Esther was in the garden behind the slave quarters walking the rows and smiling at the baby wrapped to her chest. When I approached her, I reached in my hair and from beneath the one large braid that was braided down my back, I pulled out a few seeds. I reached out my hand to her and said "I›ve been meaning to give this to you. I remember you said that this garden was full of seeds brought here from the motherland from the elder women."

"These will fit perfectly right there," she said with a smile as she took the seeds from my hand. Kneeling at the plot of soil Esther pointed out, we used our hands and our fingers to scoop out a small hole to house the seeds. Esther placed the seeds in the darkness, and we covered them with earth and patted it down. I then said to her while dusting the dirt from my hands onto my skirt apron "I need to make dinner for myself and the injured man. Is it okay if I borrow a few yams and some cabbage?"

"There's no need for that. There will be plenty with what the women are preparing now. The garden back here is for all the slaves in the quarters. We all work together to tend it. Into it we all add our seeds. It belongs to us all." The garden was arranged in rows of beautiful colors. We walked the dirt paths while pulling fresh veggies off their roots and vines. Esther then said in a hushed voice "Rachell came to me today and said you wanted to talk. I was going to stop by the cabin later, but I figure now is as good a time as any."

"Yes. Esther, I need you to do me a favor," My voice dropped to a whisper. "Esther, you›ve been here your whole life. You know the land and you know the people. Can you assist me? She looked at me seriously and without a second thought said "Absolutely, yes." She paused for a moment before saying "I know whatever is on your mind, is on my mind too."

"Who do you trust here?"

She thought for a moment and said, "I know of a few that would guard your secrets with their lives."

"My cabin at midnight, spread the word. But Esther, be sure to be discreet." She nodded in agreement, and we rejoined the group of men, women and children that were beginning to gather near the fire where tonight's meal was being prepared.

Children were running and laughing and the men were standing around talking while the women gossiped over diced vegetables and fresh meat.

All the contents went into the large cauldron that sat over the fire, filling the air with delicious aromas. One by one people walked up with their bowls to receive their ladle full of stew. Each spoonful held a rich broth filled with rice, potatoes, chicken, tomatoes, mushrooms, peppers, and onions. When each bowl was filled, all the families settled around the warm embrace of the fire.

An older man stepped slowly as he made his way towards an old tree stump by the fire. As the children settled in on long logs surrounding the flames, the older man sat and said to them "Come round here children, and old Kojo will tell you a story from the motherland."

I could tell that the old man had not been born in this new land like some of the others around us. His voice drew traces of his natural accent.

"These are the same stories the elders told me when I was just a boy in the bush. You know Kojo is an old man now."

One child smiled and said while grinning "How old are you Kojo?"

Kojo smiled and quickly said "Old as the moon." The children all laughed with mouthfuls of the hardy stew in their cheeks. They looked like jubilant little squirrels.

Kojo went on to say, "Let old Kojo tell you about a spider." The children all silenced at once and gave the old man their undivided attention.

"This spider's name was Kwaku Anansi. Now, Anansi had six sons. Their names were See-trouble, Road-builder, River-drinker, Game-skinner, Stone-thrower, and Cushion. Anansi went on a journey far away from home and got last. He found himself in grave trouble. See-trouble could sense his father was in danger and told his brothers. Road-builder said "follow me," and he crafted a path that would lead to Anansi. They found he had been swallowed by a fish, so River-drinker took a big drink, and the river was gone. Then Game-skinner stripped the fish and released Anansi. Just then, a falcon swooped down from the sky and grabbed Anansi. Stone-thrower threw a rock and hit the Falcon and Anansi fell from the sky onto his son Cushion. The spider family was so happy to be together again. Anansi was so pleased with his children that he wanted to reward them, but he did not know who deserved the prize. So, Anansi asked Nyame- the God of all things to help him decide who should be rewarded Nyame's globe of light in the sky. The brothers argued and fought all night over who should receive the prize. When Nyame saw this, he shined his light on all the sons. Kwaku Anansi knew it was because it took the strength off all the sons together to complete the task."

The kids were so excited, they yelled gleefully, "tell us another!"

I said with a grin on my face "I also have a story from the motherland." All the attention was now on me. Still grinning, I lowered my head, and in a mystical voice said, "This is a story about magic." I could see the twinkle in the eyes of the little ones as they learned in. I saw even the adults and old Kojo were listening now too. "Deep in the motherland, outside of the great river and the deep jungle, is a magical village named Elegua. In this magical village, the women could control the elements. All of nature bent to their will. The men could contort and change into animals. They embodied spirit animals and took on their likeness. They were strong and they were thunderous; and they were brave and they were proud! They lived in harmony with nature, the elements, the animals, and all that Sky Mother had created. But one day, a jealous traitor came, and he betrayed the Eleguan people. Motivated by money and power, he was tempted by an outsider who wanted to exploit the magic in the dark-skinned people. The traitor poisoned them by putting sleeping herbs in their yams. When the magical people woke up, they were shackled in chains on a slave ship in the middle of the ocean on the way to a new land. But something magical happened when they reached the shores of their new home. They discovered they still had magic. Lightning shot from the women›s fingers. The men turned into running bulls that trampled through the woods. Just like Kwaku Anansi's six sons, all the sons and daughters of the God of everything came together and used their power. And when they did, lightning struck, and trees blew in the wind, and waves of water rose high in the sky and washed away their enemies. Men flew as falcons and ran like bears as they overthrew those that betrayed them, shackled them, and enslaved them. They lived the rest of their life happily under the care of the God of all things and their magic."

One of the children looked at me and said, "Is that story really true?"

I looked in her eyes with a smile on my face and said "Yes. It is true that all those that come from the motherland harness an enate magic inside of them. No matter where they are or what happens to them, they will always have that magic."

The little girl looked back at me with wonder in her eyes and said, "I wish I could make lightning shoot from my hands" and she raised both hands high in the sky, with her fingers spread far apart as if she was releasing lightning from each of them. Just then thunder rumbled in the distance. A loud crack sounded in the sky and rain began to fall. Everyone quickly gathered their things and ran off towards their cabins, but the old man Kojo didn›t move. He sat there and stared at me with unmoving and all-knowing eyes. Before taking my leave, I looked at him and said in our native language "midnight, my cabin."

That night I left the cabin door cracked open in anticipation for those that would come. All the lights had been extinguished except for the light coming from the fire burning in the fireplace. One by one they all made their silent entry. Esther, accompanied by James, had left their baby with Nanny for the night. Behind her was James' best friend Luke. Next was Sable and Lucy, followed by Rachell and Ben. Jake came with his wife Julie, and right behind them was the stoic slave driver, John. When old man Kojo made his surprisingly quiet and swift entry into the cabin, I closed the door and locked it. I counted myself grateful to have an elder among us. Everyone found a place to sit on the floor, except for Kojo who sat in a chair nearby. No one stood, keeping in mind the windows. We sat huddled by the fire as I spoke in low whispers.

"I know you all are probably wondering why I called you here in the dark of night. I know many of you have also wondered how it came to be that I found my way here. It was not by accident, it was by choice. You see, I am no slave, and neither are you. I have been instructed by the ancestors to retrieve my family and lead them to freedom. If you so choose to join me, I have the power to equip you with what you will need to make the journey. If you stand in my way, havoc will rain down on you." I looked directly at the farmer as I spoke the words.

The silence that filled the air was charged. Kojo broke the silence by saying in his native language "is it true? the legend of the sacred lotus?" From his position atop the twin bed, the traitor answered.

"It is true, the legend of the mythical flower. This healer woman before you is the princess. And my name is not Mason. My name is Masozi of Oya, and I swear my loyalty to the princess."

I eyed the disloyal farmer. I still did not trust him, but I kept thinking back to what the cards read in Miss Dupont's deck and decided for now I was grateful for his declaration.

Esther asked, "what's he saying?" Kojo answered. "He said that the story Miss D told around the fire is true. That there is a mystical flower, and that this here is the princess, also known as the bearer of the flower."

They all stared at me as if they were seeing me for the first time.

Rachell asked "What does this mythical flower do, and how is a flower going to help us find freedom?"

John spoke up now. This was the first time I had ever heard him speak. "There is already a plan in motion that will lead us to freedom. I›ve been working with a few men on Robert Jackson's plantation. We've been planning our escape into the swamp for months now."

"Why would we escape into the swamp?" I asked curiously.

"Because there is already an established community there that is well protected," John responded.

James' deep rumbling voice added "I've heard whispers of the maroons. They say they live amongst the muddy trenches and the trees. They've figured out how to communicate with nature, and the swamp protects them from outsiders."

"And after the insurrection is complete, we will build our new home in the swamplands. All those that try to enter will be shot dead and fed to the gators." John's face was as serious as it always was. Sable cut in and said "I don›t want to live in the swamplands with the mosquitoes and the gators. I›m going North where I could live free from the fear of slavery and death."

"My mama is a slave on Robert Jackson's plantation. I will not go North without her. James and I will stay here in the swamp until our parents are rescued too," Esther replied.

Ben, now speaking for the first time, said "We should go West. I overheard a few plantation owners talking a few weeks back. They were complaining, saying that the Spanish had offered immunity and protection to all slaves that ran away and pledged their allegiance to the crown. That›s where we should go, into Spanish territory."

This was already off to a rough start. How on Earth were we supposed to come together and plan an escape if we couldn›t even decide on where we were escaping to?

Afraid the division was already beginning to settle between them, I thought to myself "what would mama do?"

In a regal tone I said to the bunch "I will not try to dictate where your path shall take you. If we work together to overthrow those who oppress us, we will be free to go whichever route we choose to go. What we need to do now is come up with a plan that will give us an open window to retrieve our families and escape. Before we put the plan into action, each person should know where they plan to end. When the task is complete, we will go our respective separate ways."

John spoke up and said "On Robert Jackson's plantation, there are two Akan warriors who were war generals in the motherland. They were sold into slavery as prisoners of wars when they were betrayed by their mistresses. They have already begun the planning of an insurrection. They have valuable information we could use to plan our escape."

"Is there a way we can arrange a meeting with them?" I asked.

John thought for a moment and replied "It is possible. If we can coordinate a time to both be in Congo Square, I can arrange for us all to meet."

Rachel then said "but master won›t let us back to Congo square unless someone is dying. He blames Miss Dupont for Franny's escape."

Ben answered "Then it is simple. We must make the master believe someone is dying. Then Lesedi will be permitted to return to Congo Square to see Miss DuPont."

"Kwame and Kofi, the Akans, are the horsemen on Robert Jackson's plantation. I travel there twice a week to exchange goods. When we have a plan, I will get a message to them that a meeting has been arranged in Congo Square by way of Miss DuPont," John replied.

"Then it is settled." Over the next hour we put our heads together to come up with a plan. We decided that it would be Rachell who would take ill. She was chosen specifically because she was Zoya's beloved daughter. Everyone knows the only person who could sway the master is his mistress. Rachell would ingest some roots that would make her violently ill. I saw the skunk roots one day when I was out picking herbs and decided they'd be good to have on hand just in case a moment like this arose. I would also give Rachell the roots that would serve as the remedy once we returned from Miss DuPont. We all commended Rachell for her bravery, as she took the role willingly. The plan would take place in a week, giving John enough time to safely get the message to Kwame and Kofi. After everyone cleared out into the darkness, including Masozi who was now healed enough to return to the fields, I sat and contemplated all that had just taken place. The plan was good enough, but I was still short of many people. The problem was we didn't know who outside of us could be trusted. It›s true many of us burn to be free, but it is also true some slaves do not wish to disrupt the normalcy of the only life they've known. We could not afford to have them jeopardize it for the others. We would make them free by burning this place to the ground and discuss it with them later. I decided to go to the small altar I'd built discreetly in a dark corner in the back of the cabin. Kneeling at the altar, I gave thanks to the mothers above. I asked that they now lead me to the men and women on this plantation they selected to be recipients of the greatest gift. That night as I slept, Mama approached me in a dream. She was dressed in cool shades of blue and white that draped all around her. Her hair laid down her back, and her brown skin shined. When she spoke, the words came out smooth as a lullaby.

"Years ago, when I first became aware of the darkness that was plaguing the villages around us, I went to the ancestors and asked them what I should do. Their response was to train the young people because a child would lead us all. Around that same time, your father and I noticed you were becoming very rebellious. I knew the ancestors were right, and they were at work. And now my daughter, I will give you the same advice the ancestors gave me. A child shall lead you. Find them and train them up in the ways."

That morning, I awakened to the sounds of the bells to begin the day. As I washed my face and prayed over my altar, I heard a knock at the door. It was Jake and his wife Julie. Jake was carrying the little girl who held her fingers to the sky last night around the fire. I opened the door and ushered them inside.

"We hate to bother you so early Miss D, but you see it's our daughter Tilly. She got bit by a snake."

The little girl was pale and slowly turning a shade of blue. I instructed them to lay her down on the bed I used for patients. Time was of the essence. The poison had to be removed before it spread any further than it already had. I saw the panic arising in Jake and Julie's face. I assured them that I had the remedy, and she would be fine. I had to lie to get them out. I told them they should go to work and return to check on Tilly later. After practically pushing them out the door, I ran over to the bedside. She was bluer now. Frantically, I ran to the wall in the back of the cabin and rubbed my hand over the grain. When I felt a change in the roughness, I gently pushed, and a hidden wood panel popped open. There the purple lotus sat glowing, all petals intact. It was the only thing that could save her now. I plucked one petal and threw it into the pot I had hanging over the fire. I then removed the pot and poured the steaming purple liquid into a small clay mug. I knew now that it was finally time. I had resisted restoring my own power for many reasons. One being I was afraid I'd fall ill again as I did with Chief Running Bull. But underneath it all I knew the real reason was because it was my last piece of home. My last piece of Mama. And even though I knew the lotus would forever serve me, the absence of a tangible piece of home filled me with deep sadness. But the ancestors led me to Tilly, and to this moment. I poured a second mug of the lotus tea. I said a prayer before pouring the liquid into the mouth of the child, and then taking a drink for myself.

The power of the tea warmed me from the inside out. I closed my eyes to indulge in the exhilarating feeling buzzing through me. When I opened my eyes, I almost couldn't believe what I was seeing. Tilly laid encased by a purple glittering glow. It had materialized all around her. I then noticed my own hands were also encased in purple light. I closed my eyes and thought of rain. My hands started moving of their own accord. Loud rain started to thunder on the roof. I smiled a true smile. The thrill of power was exhilarating. Tilly's eyes shot open. She looked at herself, and then at me, and then out of the window. I looked at her and said "Tilly, stop the rain." She closed her eyes and made a wide semicircle with her arms above her head. The rain stopped instantly. My smile was mirrored on her face. With another sweeping motion of her hands, a rainbow appeared in the sky. With wild excitement she said "Magic is real. I knew it!"

I wanted to keep Tilly close to me. Not just to study the full range of her power. There was that, but also something else. I could tell from the beginning that she was strong, and I wanted a chance to see just how strong. I could also feel myself growing stronger. Soon, it would be time to give everyone else their own tonic to restore their powers. I was suddenly having second thoughts about the group that I had selected. Remembering Mama's words to choose carefully. Was it too late now because I had already told them the plan? No. The plan could continue no one knew about the tonic and I would keep it that way for now, but Julie and Jake have a right to know.

The effect of the lotus was overpowering and draining for Tilly at first. Much like it had been for me that day at the dock. So, when Jake and Julie returned to check on her that evening she was peacefully sleeping. Julie wiped silent tears upon hearing of her daughter's recovery. Standing over her bedside, she said with eyes never leaving her child "We named her Matilda, after my older sister. I never knew my mama. She died in childbirth. My daddy fought hard to keep the three of us together after that. Matilda taught me everything my daddy couldn't. I loved her like I loved myself. Like we were the same. When I was 15, I was sold down here. Never even got an explanation why. Haven't seen my daddy or my sister since then. I was broken for a long time. But then

God gave me Jake, and he's just as good of a man as my daddy was. And then we were blessed with Tilly. Our Tilly is special. She reminds me so much of my sister."

Jake said with a smile "Tilly is a peculiar child. She is full of life and ambition. She doesn›t have the mind of a slave. She believes in everything. Julie worries about her. Says her mind is too free, and that she should have been born a man. As a man I know I shouldn't encourage such freedom in a young woman, but I love her spirit. I've never seen anything like it before."

Julie cut in, speaking with a hint of agitation she said "Jake, you can't keep on encouraging her and covering up for her. She got bit running off to play before her chores started. She's ten now, it's time for her to grow up." Jake didn't answer Julie. He turned to me and said "that›s the main reason why we're planning to run. Julie and I both know it›s only a matter of time before Tilly›s ambition spills out into the open. And around here it›s dangerous to be black with ambition, so we know that we must leave soon. Before they try to break our baby girl's spirit. I just can't have that."

The look in Julie's eyes was one of deep devotion and sadness. Jake's eyes looked equally devoted, but in the place of sadness was a look of eagerness. I could tell Julie loved her husband and her daughter fiercely. And even though she seemed to be the least ambitious of the three, I knew she would protect them with her life. While Jake and Tilly were free spirits, Julie was born a protector. Julie never wanted for herself, only for her family, and she'd kill the master himself if she had to in order to protect them. Jake knew that, and in turn loved his wife even more than she loved him. Jake looked at his daughter as if she were all the things that Julie wasn›t allowed to be. Julie had fear put into her a long time ago, but their darling Tilly was born fearless.

I decided at that moment to restore Jake and Julie first. I knew I was making the right decision. As I rose to ready myself, I heard some scratching at the door and a few whimpers and cries. Julie said aloud "Jake that dog swears she's your daughter too. Can't stand to be outside without ya."

Jake laughed and said to me, "it's my hound, Belle."

I smiled. Jake had a spirit animal already, and he hadn't even been restored. "Let her in," I said with a smile.

When Jake opened the door, a reddish-brown hunting dog strolled inside and sat at the bedside of Tilly. Although sitting, she remained alert, looking back and forth between Tilly and her master. As Jake knelt to pet the faithful dog, he said "one of my jobs here on the plantation is training the dogs. Most of the dogs used by masters are bloodhounds, but this dog in particular is a coonhound. Master bought her by accident. At first glance, they look like bloodhounds, but the trained eye could tell the difference. She's a good girl. Best hunter of the pack honestly, and the only coonhound in a pack of bloodhounds."

Julie musingly said "that dog once was more trouble than she was worth. I recall a time all the slaves was lined up for breakfast. The dog came and got in line with Jake. She waited patiently by his side as if it was time for her breakfast too! She would stay by Jake's side despite the yells of the overseer. One day, the overseer struck the poor dog with a rock. Got tired of her disobedience to him, and her loyal obedience to a slave. Poor Belle whimpered off, and Jake was miserable the entire day. Swore to me then and there he'd have his revenge one day on that overseer Wayne for striking his beloved Belle. When the bells rang at the end of the day, we found her waiting right outside the cabin. And from that day on, Belle's allegiance was not to the masters that used her, but to the black man who raised her. And it seems as though she has some influence over the other dogs as well, because the bloodhounds followed her lead. They would only participate in a hunt if instructed to by my Jake. But the master won't get rid of the dogs, says they're the most well-trained dogs he's ever seen. Gives the credit to my Jake. Even rents him out to other plantations from time to time to help train their animals. It just shows that Jake's the best hound trainer in all of Louisiana." Julie beamed as she bragged about her husband. Jake tried to hide the glee in his face, but it was bright as the sun. The love they shared was a power in itself.

Jake replied "it's my Julie that keeps me strong. All that good cooking could bring a man back from the dead." Julie's cheeks turned a shade of pink, making her look very much like Tilly. Tilly was a slightly round little girl with chubby, rosy red cheeks. Her size was an outward show of her mother and father's devotion to her. Her skin was the same shade of golden wheat as Julie's. She wore long braided pigtails that hung to her shoulders. Julie often wrapped the long pigtails braids into circled knots on top of each side of her head. She was such a cute and innocent little girl.

I grabbed a piece of smoked meat I had in the pantry, given to me by Esther and James, and held out a small piece, summoning the pretty red hound. When she came and ate out of my hand, I stroked her coat and said to Julie and Jake "I must share with you the truth about your Tilly. The truth is when you brought her to me, she could not be saved. The venom had spread too quickly. To save her, I had to use a special plant I brought with me from home. This plant restored her health, but also other things she may not have known she ever had to lose in the first place. It won't harm her in any way, only make her stronger. I would like to share the same with you if you're ready. It will not harm you, only enhance what you naturally have."

"That day at the fire, Tilly kept saying you gave her magic. She said she made the rain. Me and Julie laughed but, it's true, isn't it?"

"The story I told was true, but I cannot account for the rain. That is between Tilly and Sky Mother."

"You saved our girl," Julie said plainly. "If this will help us be free, I'm all in."

Jake beamed and said "yea, me too."

I smiled and stood from my chair. Floating through the room, I poured the tea and lit some candles, suddenly feeling my spirits lifted. I said a whispered prayer as I handed Jake and Julie their mugs. Julie smiled and said "cheers» as they clinked their mugs together and took a slow sip. A purple luminescent glow soon encased them both before leaving them and turning into a purple glittery haze throughout the room.

Belle howled, and Jake's eyes shot to her, wide with disbelief. A smile just as wide as his eyes slowly spread across his face. "You can understand me girl, can't you?" he said looking down at the dog. When Belle happily barked Jake shot to his feet and happily danced with Belle who stood up on her hind legs. Julie looked on in a state of shock. In the corner, Tilly had awakened and was now also smiling at her dancing dad and his canine companion.

Julie had not moved or spoken. I put my hand atop hers and said "it's ok. Close your eyes. Tap in with yourself," Julie closed her eyes. She took a few deep breaths, taking her time before reopening her eyes. When she finally opened her eyes, her brown irises were glowing like sunshine through molasses. She focused her attention on a large potted plant in the corner. When she punched her two fists together, the soil from the plant materialized in the air. Following the direction of her hand movements, the soil took every form she did. When she mimicked a rounding motion, it compacted into a ball and slowly landed in her open palms. Not one speck of dirt hit the ground. She released the sphere, and it floated back into the pot on the floor.

Julie looked at her hands with disbelief as Jake and Tilly cheered. Belle was howling too.

"Mama, that was amazing!" Tilly cheered from the bed. A smile finally cracked Julie's face.

When Belle barked, Jake said in response "Yea, I'm hungry too. What's for dinner? We should celebrate!"

"Now hold on, Jake. We've got to be careful. If this got around,

Master would have us sold by morning! We have to be smart and discreet. Just keep doing everything the same as we always do."

"Julie's right," I said seriously. I do encourage you to get to know your power. The gifts that we receive are sacred and personal. Your journey to learning the full spectrum of your power is yours alone. Learn how to use it, but please do so discreetly. Your life and your freedom depend on it." A serious feeling had overtaken the jubilance that filled the room just a few short seconds ago. "Well, I must admit I am hungry too. We'll eat in our own cabin today. I want to test out a new recipe," Julie said as she smiled at Jake. He smiled back lovingly. "Miss Lesedi, you're welcome to join us for dinner tonight, or any night for that matter," Julie said warmly. I respectfully declined tonight but told her I planned on stopping by one day soon. After a lot of hugs, and a few goodbyes, Jake carried Tilly on his back and the family of four headed out into the sunset.

# CHAPTER 13 *LESEDI*

O ver the next few days, there was much to keep me busy. I found that gossip between the workers held a wealth of information. It was the enslaved Africans job to know all the inner workings of the plantation. Their owner's arrogance and ignorance towards the thinking abilities of the uneducated slaves hindered them from accepting the fact the workers heard every whisper and every conversation. Over dinner with Jake, Julie and Tilly, Julie filled me in about some of the things going on around here. She spoke in a hushed tone as she recalled the story.

In her sweet southern accent, she said "it seems as though when the root woman Franny was still on the plantation, Master would let her go into the quarter to see Miss DuPont. When Sally found out she was carrying the overseer's baby, Master was so excited. Every baby born into slavery is a slave master didn't have to purchase, you see. Word is Sally and her husband, a slave named Jacque, went to Franny, and asked her to get rid of the baby. She said it was a demon and she'd kill herself before she bore it. So, Franny went to see Miss DuPont. When she returned, she had some roots for Sally to chew on. The next day, Sally went to bed, and we all knew why. After that, Miss DuPont suggested we hang morning glory vines outside our cabins, and we all did so. When they bloomed, the cabins were surrounded by bees. We used smoke and fire to navigate through the bees at first. Eventually the bees avoided us slaves all together. It was a good tactic for keeping unwanted visitors out. A few weeks later, Franny disappeared, and Sally and Jacque were gone with her. Master was furious. Said he lost four slaves in one month, because he counted the unborn baby as property as well. It got rough around here after that for a while. The whispers say Miss DuPont's grandmother was an Akan warrior and voodoo priestess who was captured in Africa and sold into slavery after an enemy cursed her. When her master suddenly died under curious circumstances, people quickly believed there was some magic involved. The masters were worried that Africans coming into slavery brought with them secrets of magic from the mother continent that have been stripped from the generations of Africans born into slavery. They started to warn us about what they called 'black magic', saying that it was of the devil and evil. It was their fear of slaves using their native spiritual magic for liberation, because it would undermine the foundation of white supremacy that they›ve built. But the whispers in the slave cabins told a different story. The whispers in the slave cabins said that the magic was pure, and that it was of good and of spirit. That the magic we could possess could empower us and liberate us. But if the masters got word that any of the slaves were practicing any other religion besides Christianity, they would make an example out of that slave. So magic was forced to be done in private and in secrecy. Lucy prays to Catholic Saints that are really her African spirit guides. She disguises them. So, I›ve always known magic was real. If I›m honest, I›d have to say deep down I was always a little afraid of its power. But I always knew it was out there. And then when Tilly was born, that›s all she could talk about. Jake and I never filled Tilly with silly thoughts of grandeur, but Tilly would see magic in her dreams. She would tell Jake and I what she saw, and we would be in awe. We knew from the time she was little she was different. I›d like to thank you, Miss Lesedi, for what you›re doing here. We›ll be careful. We recognize how dangerous it all is, but Jake and I believe that the magic is much stronger."

Listening to Julie's story made me painfully aware of just how many Africans had been stolen, and how long it'd been happening. The fact that I grew up blissfully unaware, comfortable in the walls of my village filled me with guilt and unease. And even though I was so glad to have the information, the reality of it made my heart sink like bricks in the river. I went back to my cabin that night and tried to concentrate on the coming plans. Everything was in order. The plan was concrete. With that in place and no other plan to focus on now, I found myself slipping deeper and deeper into sadness and darkness.

I'd busied myself with work around the plantation to keep myself from thinking about how much I missed them all. I didn't want to think about how I would never see my Mama again, and the possibility that I also might not ever see my Baba again. I wondered what Nia and Ife's life would be like if they were still together. Would we be having a wedding right now? Celebrating and dancing at our sacred center? I think about my auntie Abeena and her young son. How they joined the ocean after he had only just begun to live. He did not even know himself. Was death the better option? My Mama Oni who is old now will never know what became of me. It makes me so angry. I have never felt an anger this strong. Its fury burns my lungs. I have all these thoughts now that I never had before. When life was good, I only wanted peace, happiness, and adventure, but now life is hard. I still want happiness, but now I want it at the expense of those who stole it from me. I want to see them suffer. I want to see them beg. I want to rip everything out of them that they ripped from me. I don't know who I am anymore. I wasn't raised this way, but this world is not what I imagined it to be. I am so far from the woman I once was. If my Mama heard me speak this way, what would she think of me?

I find that it is easier than I thought to pretend that everything is okay. Not knowing who to trust helps build the walls needed to protect your inner self. However, I find that the fire inside of you gets hotter and hotter every time you have to tell that same lie. Day after day. I am slowly blazing from the inside out. And although I have made great friends who I love like family here, I spend most of my days alone stuck in my head. Stuck in my thoughts of the past, riddled with regrets and confusion. I don't know which way is up. My body moves on its own accord, my brain in too much turmoil to direct it. I try to steady myself. This plan with Rachell would require my full attention. Her life she so bravely volunteered hangs in the balance. One wrong move and it could all be over. It was early fall now, and even though most families decided to eat in their cabins, there was still always dinner, stories, and laughter around the fire behind the slave quarters. Tonight, there was music playing. Someone was strumming a string instrument and there was clapping and singing heard in the distance. I sat at the table alone in my cabin and ate the same porridge I've eaten every day for the last few weeks. It's the first recipe my grandmother taught me to cook back home. I've been so homesick I've made it every day. Although missing several ingredients that are native to home, I've found substitutions here that seem to work almost just as well. The sweet potatoes for example are a welcome replacement for the yams I miss so dearly. As I ate in silence, I heard a knock on the door.

"Hey Lesedi, it's me Esther. Can I come in?" I opened the door to a petite and light brown smiling woman with her hair wrapped perfectly in a worn faded blue cloth, and her baby strapped to her with larger pieces of the same worn blue fabric that was on her head.

"Hadn't seen you around lately. Figured I'd check in on you and make sure you didn't need anything."

I looked at her with sad and grateful eyes. I'd been drowning for so long, I forgot how good it feels to have someone check on you. I'd been missing that since I left home.

"Thank you," I said humbly. "I miss my family." My eyes were unable to meet hers. I felt weak and hopeless, and honestly embarrassed. I come from women who never showed signs of weakness. Feeling so succumbed to my emotions made me feel as if I failed all those women who raised me. Esther looked at me sympathetically.

"You know, after Master sold my Mama, I was angry for a long time. Except I wasn't as good as you at controlling it. It seemed to spill out of me every which way. I remember the day an older slave woman slapped me for saying out loud that I was going to run away and find freedom. I went back to Nanny so upset. I was crying and hysterical. Nanny said to me you got to be smart, girl. I›m gonna give you the keys to your freedom. And then she pulled out this here Bible." Esther reached into her apron and pulled out a small worn book.

"That was the day Nanny started teaching me how to read. Pretty soon I couldn›t stop. I'd hide on the floor and flip through the pages by candlelight. I'd read every story and every passage. What I learned was God always gives us signs. Signs are all around us because God created everything around us. If you learn to listen with your eyes, and see with your ears, Mother Nature will reveal God's will to you. I'd like to read something to you if you don't mind."

''No not at all, please do," I replied sincerely. She flipped through the pages of the worn bible while saying "Psalms has always been my favorite, but I think you could benefit from the story of Job. I've been reading about Job lately. Job is a man that is constantly tested throughout his life. He endured much pain and heartbreak, but he never allowed himself to believe that God would abandon him. He had God's favor. When his suffering passed, he was blessed with overflow, more than he could have ever dreamed. It says here '*But ask the animals, and they will teach you, or the birds in the sky, and they will tell you; or speak to the earth, and it will teach you, or let the fish in the sea inform you.*

*Which of all these does not know that the hand of the Lord has done this? In his hand is the life of every creature and the breath of all mankind.'*

I know all I›m doing is repeating to you things that you already know, but sometimes you just need to hear it from a friend. God is all around us. And the signs are all around us. When I was praying for a way out, God delivered straight to me a magic African princess with a plan for freedom. So even though you may not see it now, I know that this is all a part of his plan. And I know you miss your family. That›ll never change, but I hope you find some comfort in knowing that God is always with you. I'm with you too. We're soul sisters." She smiled big and nudged me a little with love. I couldn't help but smile, so grateful in this moment for the gift of sisterhood. When a single tear escaped, she came over and wrapped her arms around me. The power of her rehabilitating hug brought out a cascade of tears. She rubbed my back while saying "if you wake my baby, you're putting her back to sleep." I laughed through the tears, feeling my spirit instantly lifted.

"Lilly actually has no problem sleeping. It's me that has been having trouble lately." She instinctively put one hand to her belly, before removing it. One look in her eyes showed the fear that she dared not say. She was carrying, and afraid of what that might mean once the master found out. I could assume by what Julie told me about the master's view of what his "property" was, that Esther felt the impending threat to her family's freedom.

Before she departed for the night, I said to her "I think this may be another one of your signs, Esther. It just so happens that I have some special tea that I've been holding on to. I'm sure it'll help with your insomnia. Why don't you take some back with you and share it with James. Then the two of you come back and see me tomorrow." After preparing the brew in a small cauldron for Esther to carry back with her, we exchanged thanks, hugs, and then goodbyes. That night at the altar, I thanked the mothers for sisterhood. I had never had a sister biologically, but my life was full of strong women who shared their strength with me and protected us all without us even knowing it. Evidence of that was Rachell's sacrifice for the progression of our plan. Tonight, was the night she would take the skunk root. I was anxious for the morning after. I knew it was only a matter of time before frenzy reached my doorstep.

It was common knowledge that Rachell was fiercely protective over her brother Ben. In her own life, her situation was not as bad as his, but sometimes the biggest struggle you're facing isn't your own, it's your brother's. And it's our duty to help carry the load of those we love. Rachell is driven by her desire to see her brother live a happier life. She wants him to thrive. She worries about him. She told me the day I gave her the roots that God blessed her brother with physical strength and her with strength of the mind. She had always been able to think clearly in adversity, something Ben could not do. His plans were more often than not ill-prepared and erratic. He was strong and powerful in the fields, but his mind was like straw, not stable enough to hold balance. He tried to work though the darkness in his mind but having lacked a foundation of love in his life has made him weak. So, she decided she would be his protector. Even when he doesn't know she is protecting him. And she's happy to do it. Happy to see her brother have one less thing to worry about.

As predicted, Zoya was inconsolable over Rachell suddenly taking ill. I wondered if she would have shown the same compassion for Ben. Something told me she would not have, and something also told me Ben knew it too. When he reported to us Zoya's uneasy state, I could sense a tinge of sadness in him too. Zoya insisted we leave at first light in pursuit of the infamous Miss Dupont.

# CHAPTER 14 *LESEDI*

The next morning, Zoya was at my door before the sun rose, a sleepy master Andre Rousseau in tow. She spoke shakily but firmly as she urged John and I into the wagon. The grass was covered in dew, and the sun was creating an orange glow in the dark blue distance. The horse's gallop and the wheels of the wagon drummed in rhythm as the cool morning air filled my lungs. I stared into the dissipating darkness as we made our way into the now awakening Congo square.

The trek that morning was a muddy one. It had rained all night making the journey longer than before. By the time we arrived at Monique's, the rain had re-emerged. Stepping through the back door, we made our way into a side parlor room. Inside were whom I assumed to be the Akan warriors Kwame and Kofi. They demanded your attention with their stature. Tall and wide, I was sure they had to duck to fit inside the doorframe. They were both dark brown with the biggest muscles I'd ever seen. Like statuesque gorillas that ruled their jungle. They didn't smile. They barely spoke, and when they did it was in their native language. They stood there, still as soldiers, with their arms folded across their chests and their stance wide.

Seated at the table with his fingers interlaced was a light skin man with fire in his eyes. He was thin and muscular with thick veins in his massive hands and arms. He wore a thick mustache and a bearded face that made him look both homely and dangerous. Atop his head was a bushel of brown curls. This man was hard to read, and I could tell that was by design. Monique said in her creole drawl "Lesedi, let me introduce you to Charles."

"Pleased to meet you," I said as John, Monique and I took our seats at the table. He did not respond. Instead, he tilted his head towards me before saying "Miss DuPont says I can trust you. She says you, an African healer slave woman, will be the general of the Rousseau plantation. I wanted to see for myself why the cards chose a woman," He stared at me as if he was waiting for me to answer.

"I am not a slave," I snapped before I could stop myself. "That is only my current position. I am the daughter of great African chiefs, and I lead my people even now. Healing is just one of the many things I can do," I replied, placing heat behind my words.

He looked at me with cold eyes that did not soften as Monique smiled.

"Well, queen, I hope one of the things you do well is rebel." The smile he offered did not reach his eyes. It almost looked twisted and threatening.

"I know you are new here, queen, but I'm sure you have realized by now that it is the slaves that are the life and breath of every plantation. We possess the skills, the strength and the knowledge that brings in the money. What I have realized as a driver is that the white man will tell us that we are not valuable, when we indeed are priceless. You see, without us Africans, none of this happens. Without us no money is made, and when there is no money, there is no society. My plan is to burn it all to the ground and build a new society where we Africans, the descendants of great queens and kings, take our rightful place among the people, which is on top."

The room was still and thick with silence. Charles continued to speak uninterrupted. His face closely resembled an African cobra's, and his words were its venom.

"Soon it will be the holiday season. Thanksgiving followed by Christmas followed by Carnival. The white men here get fat and drunk for months straight, and we slaves make sure business goes on as usual because we are the brains and the muscle of the entire operation! While they stuff their faces, we work the land and live off crumbs through the winter. But this year, that will all change. You see, while they're busy drinking and eating and fornicating, we will be building.

Each plantation shall build its own army. We already have an army on the Andrews' plantation. The master Andrew uses their plantation as a warehouse for the local militia. We have already secured a place to stash seeds, uniforms, guns, and ammunition after we ransack the stores. We will start on the Andrews land, and march from plantation to plantation, increasing our army and burning down everything in our path. As we increase our ranks we will march towards the quarter and take New Orleans by storm. We will claim this city as the new Africa. Ran by us, the way God intended."

I listened carefully and silently, now realizing that the general and I had two totally different visions of what life we wanted for our people. I thought I wanted to burn down this place just as much as the general did, but upon hearing his plan something just didn't sit right with me about it. Yes, I want freedom for my people and yes, I wanted the people responsible for our bondage to pay, but the thought of burning down plantation after plantation made me uneasy.

So instead, I asked "and what are we to do about those who choose not to fight? The people who choose not to be a part of the army, and not to storm New Orleans?"

"We make them. If they refuse, we dispose of them," he responded bluntly. "We cannot afford to have a traitor among us. Our positions are too delicate. Either you go free, or you die. What is slavery but a slow death anyway?"

I just stared at him, not knowing how to respond.

"Your job queen is to weed out the weak. Once we are building an army, we can only use men and women who are strong. Any message you wish to pass to me you can send through John, and I will do the same. We plan to strike right after Christmas. That is when they are most vulnerable. When they are fat and warm living off what we worked for. From now until then I expect you to compose your army and allocate weapons. Whatever you can use, hoes, rakes, shovels, knives. We have already trained our slaves with guns, bow and arrows, and shovels. Their love of money, luxury and debauchery will be the death of them."

When the secret meeting was over Charles and the Akans left first. John and I waited for a while before leaving, being careful not to cause any unwanted attention. On our way out, Monique pulled me inside a hidden doorway and closed the door. The room was dark with candles lit everywhere. Monique's bright brown face glowed in the candlelight although she seemed to be surrounded by shadows. "How has your search been going?" she asked.

"Slow, but good. I've found the ones I trust to be solid." She nodded her approval before saying "He does not believe the cards. He plans to go against the ancestors' wishes, therefore his arrogance will be his demise. The ancestors are calling for action, but it must be balanced. To have balance, you need the power of the masculine and the feminine. A man and woman, working side by side with the same vision. Charles told you your job was to weed out the weak, and he was incorrect. The ancestors have already done so. Your job in addition to finding your flower bearers is to balance the energy. You carry the divine feminine energy of the great mothers, but that is all you carry. You are missing an intricate piece, which is the mighty flow of the masculine fathers. Everything is created in balance, made to be defined by its opposite. Kings and queens were made to be equal. They share equally their strength and weakness, and their joy and pain. Balancing each other out the way the ancestors intended. Let them lead you to your balance, so you can lead our people to theirs."

My mind raced as we rode back to the plantation following our meeting with the general. He made valid points. One could not deny that Africans were the very backbone of the same society we are excluded from. But there were so many holes in the general's plan. Thinking about it now, I wonder if he had really thought it through, or if his anger has blinded him. If we really succeeded in taking over, how would we sustain? How could we rebuild the city that we burned down and defend ourselves from invasion at the same time? It took me no time to realize that the general's plan would get us all killed but remembering his condescending words *why the cards chose a woman* told me immediately that he had the mindset of the men Kendi used to tell me about in her village. A thought that Miss DuPont confirmed. Those men who deemed themselves smarter than us women and took it upon themselves to delegate what life should be for us. I wondered how I, a woman new to this land, could convince men who had served as generals and soldiers in another time that their plan would lead us all to a bloody death. Surely, they will look at me as a childish woman I thought. I had nothing to demand their respect or their attention. How would I make them listen to me? I knew that I should be the leader of this insurrection. I knew that with me in charge all our people have their best hope of survival. Not that I had all the answers, but I had connections to the ancestors. I had a connection to higher forces, to higher powers that will surely keep us safe. And one thing that I knew for sure was that death and destruction was never Sky Mother's way. It put me in a precarious position that I had never found myself in before. I never dreamed that there would come a time I questioned all my values, and everything I learned. I had been taught that death, greed, and destruction were evil, and that we were to be as kind as Sky Mother is. Now I see that when you are faced with such a great evil, it takes something even stronger to bring it down. I remembered Chief Running Bull's words about power in numbers when the fight is between the equally powerful water and fire. If we are water, then we must be greater than fire. All of us together could win if we used our powers for good, but it seemed as though the general was intent on fighting fire with fire.

And if we didn't get behind him, he would be ready to burn us down too. Between now and the holidays, I would have to figure out how to assemble my own army and how to deal with the general. And then I thought over Monique's words, about finding my balance. Honestly the thought of it seemed impossible and unattainable. But the words "mighty flow of masculine power" stuck to the back of my mind.

When we arrived back at the plantation, we went directly to Rachell. She was sweaty and moaning in her cabin with her worried mother by her side. Upon seeing us enter, her mother breathed a sigh of relief. I quickly busied myself preparing the remedy for Rachell. After medication, she peacefully dozed into sleep. I informed Zoya that with rest, her beloved daughter would return to herself within a day. Zoya departed to give master Andre the news. What neither Zoya nor Rachell knew was that I had given Rachell more than just the remedy for the skunk root. I also gave her the tonic of the Lotus. When she recovered, she would be stronger than she remembered. Stronger than she ever knew she was. I whispered in her ear "when you get your strength back come see me. Don›t you forget." She nodded and peacefully pulled her quilt higher, as her breathing steadied at a serene pace.

I spent the rest of my day helping with chores around the plantation. Off in the distance, I saw Jake in the fields. In front of him were a dozen dogs all sitting at attention and looking directly at him. The sight made me smile both inside and out.

Tilly was among the other children pulling worms and other insects from the dirt that threatened the crops. I noticed although the sun was ablaze in the midday sky, Tilly seemed to have the cool shade of a cloud above her. Upon seeing me walk by, she smiled brightly and with her eyes directed me to look up at the cloud above her. I smiled and winked at her as I continued on my path.

I headed over the large basins to help Lucy and a few other women with laundry, which was not easy work. The lye was so rough, it would crack your skin. Lucy's hands and feet were a permanent shade of bluish purple, evidence of her time working as a slave on an indigo plantation. Her hands were dark, dyed, and cracked. Over the steam of the hot water, I said to Lucy "come see me later, I have some aloe and almond oil for your hands." She smiled and replied "That would be lovely, thank you. I collect pecans off the trees out back. I'll bring you a few in return for your kindness." I gave her hand a squeeze, flashed a smile, and quickly got back to work as I noticed overseer Wayne's surly gaze from a distance.

When the day's work was over, I headed back to my cabin, not surprised at all to see Esther sitting on the steps with one leg shaking. As I approached her, she quickly stood up and walked towards me at a hurried pace.

"Lesedi, what was in that tea you gave us last night?"

With a huge grin I replied "why, is something wrong?"

In a hushed voice, Esther moved in closer to me and whispered "I think I moved water with my hands today. And James, well um. Maybe you better come see for yourself." Taking my hand, Esther led me behind the cabins, past the garden to a gathering of trees. Standing on two feet in the clearing was the biggest black bear I've ever seen. He was picking berries intricately with his meaty paws.

"James!" Esther yelled in a whisper. The bear quickly snapped his head our way. Within an instance, his black fur morphed into black skin. He ran over to us, moving at lightning speed. When he reached us, he said "you know, I would have chosen a dragon, but a bear is not bad." He smiled a big white smile that lit up his handsome face before saying "show her Esther."

"I can't, not here!" she replied in that same hushed yell as she started off back towards my cabin quickly. Once we stepped inside, Esther looked around. When she spotted a pitcher of water on the table she froze.

James encouraged her by chanting "do it, Esther! Do it, do it!" while grinning like a mischievous young boy. Finally, Esther looked at her husband, rolled her eyes, and smiled. She took her right index finger and spun it around in a circling motion. As she did, the water in the pitcher rose into the air and spun in circles. When she flicked all five of her fingers open, the water droplets separated and lingered in the air like small pockets of floating bubbles. On Esther's face was pure joy as she watched the droplets dance. James watched her as he stared at her happy face with doting eyes. Esther, looking like she was suddenly hit by unpleasantness, face sunk, and the water splashed to the floor. She looked at James, whose face now looked concerned. Before anyone could speak, Esther said, "will my baby have powers?"

James asked curiously "You gave Lilly tea?"

"I wasn't talking about Lilly, but now that I think about it, I'm nursing her, so will she have it too?"

James's jaw dropped open as he stood to embrace his wife.

"I knew it! You've been snoring like a bear lately," he gushed with the widest smile on his face. He moved in with his arms wide, and Esther fell into them like a sleepy child. When she rested her head on his chest, he rocked her while hugging her tightly and saying, "God has truly blessed me."

Esther looked up into James' face and asked, "you're not scared Master will take the baby from us?"

"You forget I'm a dangerous black bear. I can protect you now. All of you." He placed an open palm on Esther's disguised belly. Esther smiled and laid her head back on James' massive chest. For a moment I think they forgot I was there, because they looked startled when I said, "To answer your question, Esther, I'm not sure about the babies, but I think there's a good chance that they might."

Later that evening, Lucy stopped by. We sat down at the table together and just talked for a while. She told me about her life in South Carolina and how she worked dying fabric in indigo day in and day out for the first half of her life. When her master found out that she could read he sold her down the river, away from everything and everyone she'd ever known. Lucy was quiet and reserved. Her skin was dark, and her hair was short and thick. Her lips and nose were wide, and her almond shaped eyes and long eyelashes sparkled. Lucy and I decided to join the many people who were now starting to gather outside around the fire for dinner. It was the weekend, and Master had given the slaves permission to roast a whole hog. Men and women were outside working together to prepare the meal. The sweet, savory, and smokey smells of the pork dripping over the fire was beginning to attract a crowd. On our way, we ran into John. The usually stoic slave driver took one look at Lucy and seemed to have forgotten who he was. He stuttered and stammered while saying "good evening miss Lucy. You look mighty beautiful tonight." He took his hat off and placed it to his chest, giving her a small bow. I had never seen John like this. Lucy seemed to have him tripping all over himself. As we made our way to an empty log and waited for what was being served, I said to Lucy "I think John may be sweet on you."

"Nooooo," she said smiling. "Do you really think so?"

"Well, I›m no expert on love, and I can›t say that he told me, but Esther told me to start listening with my eyes. And if I heard him correctly, by the way he was looking at you, girl, he's head over heels," I gushed. Lucy blushed and gave a shy smile. Just then we heard a deep voice clearing its throat behind us.

"Umm, excuse me ladies, I don›t mean to interrupt. I just wanted to ask Miss Lucy if she would like to accompany me on a short walk?" Lucy looked up and said, "Well I did make plans to spend my evening with my dear friend Miss Lesedi, but you are welcome to join us."

John smiled and replied "well thank you. I think I will."

Dinner around the fire quickly turned into a secret reunion as Rachell and Ben came to join us. Upon seeing Rachell, we could not contain our excitement. We were all so happy to see that she had made a full recovery and that our plan was successful. Rachell walked up and hugged me. Then she looked me in my eyes and hugged me a second time, this time whispering in my ear "I know what you did, and it›s our secret."

I smiled at her and said "Lucy and John are gonna join me for some tea. You›re welcome to come by if you'd like.

Rachell quickly replied "Oh yes, I›m coming. I›ll bring some sweet potato pie. I made one earlier."

"I›ve never had sweet potato pie before, but it sounds delicious!" I was honestly really excited about that pie.

It was Saturday night, and the slave quarters were filled with talking, laughing, music, drinking, and dancing. Sunday was the only day the slaves had off and we made the most of it. As the night went on, more and more of the friends I'd made showed up around the fire. Before long, what started out as a few friends reuniting, turned into loud conversations, laughs, and even some cursing with Esther, James, Luke, Julie, Jake, Lucy, John, and Sable now joining us. When dinner was over, we all decided to go back to my cabin, as I had the most space, and we were having what seemed like the most fun since I arrived. What began as tea with Lucy turned into whiskey, red beans and rice, and sweet potato pie with the whole gang. Rachell told stories of pranks she played in the house as a child on the master and his deceased wife, recalling once placing the fingers of the sleeping mistress in warm water while she slept. When she woke up, she was so embarrassed she peed straight through her gown and sheets, that she blamed it on the master and demanded he purchase new fabric. Rachell laughed while saying "and at the age of seven I learned a valuable lesson: Although the pranks were genius and hilarious, all they did was make more work for the slaves."

A slightly tipsy Julie replied "boo! We never get to have any fun."

"I don›t know, baby. Lately I›ve been enjoying life," Jake said with a wide grin.

Julie said a little bit slurred "you know what, Jake? Me too, and it›s all thanks to Miss D. To Miss D!" she said while holding her mug in the air.

All the friends in the cabin echoed "To Miss D." as mugs clanked.

147

Esther was the only one drinking water.

Lucy said excitedly "Well I know we are all glad to have you here."

"Yes, and we are all glad that you have the knowledge that you have," Julie added while indiscreetly winking.

Lucy looked at her and laughed as she turned her face up and asked "Julie, why are you winking like that?"

Julie replied, "I can›t tell you Lucy, cause it›s a secret."

Jake put his hand to his forehead and just shook his head. I couldn›t help but laugh. Julie turned to her husband and said "what you doing all that for Jake? I didn›t tell her!"

"Does everybody here know something that I don›t?" John looked at Lucy and said, "I›m starting to wonder myself if I›ve missed something."

"You shall know soon enough. Let›s have some tea. We›ve had a lot of whiskey. The tea will help settle us."

"Good idea," Jake said, eyeing his shrugging wife. Julie just laughed and snorted. Sable, who was watching her with glee, said, "Whatever the secret, it must be a good one."

James replied in his deep voice "It might be the best secret I›ve ever kept."

"Luckily for all of you that are here, we will share the secret together. We are family now, and I believe that each of you has been uniquely made. I am so grateful to have met you all, and I will always carry you with me," I said.

I stepped into the back room and returned with one petal of the Lotus, the third one that I had used. It glowed in my hand. Everyone looked at me silently. "This is the Lotus from the story. It holds powerful magic, but it is rare. This is the only flower that was here at the beginning. The women in my family have protected this flower for generations, but I have been instructed by the ancestors to use the flower's restorative powers to give you what was taken from you. Some of you have already had its tea. The rest of you that have not, the time is now."

I grabbed a few cups and handed them to their owners- Lucy, John, Sable, and Luke. For some reason, Ben had declined to join us. Rachell, who was used to Ben's lack of social interaction , hadn't thought twice about it. Looking at the rest of my friends sitting around the table with empty cups, I suddenly had the urge to do something I›ve never done before; something I had only seen my grandmother do. I closed my eyes and thought about her, and when I opened my eyes, I waved my hand

149

over the cauldron hanging over the fire. The same purple mist that I saw my grandmother create so many times appeared with the same smell of lavender and chamomile. A sweeping sensation took over me: the realization that I could not fully process what just happened. I just knew that I had tapped into my grandmother's essence, and I was grateful. Looking up, I realized everyone in the room was also looking at me. I smiled and poured each empty cup with the purple liquid and then we all drank together. As purple light started to fill the room, we all looked around at the transformations that were being made.

Sable had completely disappeared. Her body was invisible, replaced with a cool breeze that you could feel when she was near. Luke's long lean frame transformed into a huge, long, wide, and glossy black spider. He began quickly weaving intricate webs. When a rocking chair suddenly appeared in the corner, seeming to be only made of glossy silver fibers, we looked on in astonishment. When it was John's turn to showcase his gift, he closed his eyes. When they reopened, they were wide and yellow with deep dark centers like an owl's. His neck turned his head almost completely around. He said in a low voice, "my eyes, I could see all the way into the big house. It's like I have the vision of a spyglass."

Julie, who had obviously been testing her abilities, made motions towards the same potted plant in the corner. This time, instead of dirt rising, flowers instantly bloomed. Gorgeous red roses with long thick needle like thorns that were as sharp as broken glass. The rose bush was enchanting and dangerous, truly a reflection of Julie.

James' spirit animal, the black bear, gifted him with super strength and speed. When they asked him to show his power, he laid back in his chair with his legs spread wide and one arm around his wife.

"It's nothing really. I just turn into a terrifying, ferocious black bear. This room ain't big enough for me."

He cracked a sly smile and Esther rolled her eyes, trying her hardest not to smile. Then he stood up and picked up the entire chair with Esther in it with one hand. With his free hand, he lifted the chair opposite side him with the sitting long and lanky Luke still in. He lifted them up and down effortlessly before putting them down and saying "this is light work" with a smile. Esther smirked at her husband and moved her pointer figure sharply. Steaming hot liquid levitated from the cauldron atop the fire and slithered like a snake to the wave of her finger. The steaming liquid moved seductively as did Esther›s hand. James starred with his mouth slightly open and lips twisted into a grin. When the liquid found its way to the cup in front of James, it poured down like a steamy waterfall.

"Woooo! Alright now, Esther!" The women in the room cat called to her as her husband stared at her with googly eyes. I was excited to see what Rachell would show, as I had not seen her gift yet. When it was her turn, she said "okay, I think maybe y'all should stand back for this." Rachell stood up, and we all moved our chairs back a few feet. She closed her eyes and placed her hands at her sides, palms up. When she blinked her eyes open, her wild red hair had turned into dancing fire. Her eyes glowed red. She slowly lifted her palms and small spheres of fire circled above them. When she closed her eyes again. All the fires disappeared. Her wild red hair returns to frizzy curls.

"Rachell!! I always knew you were a firecracker!" Sable jeered and we all laughed. Julie nudged Jake and said, "Gone on, show 'em baby."

"Alright, alright," Jake said as he stood up. His tall and muscular frame began transforming into a beautiful black and brown rottweiler. His fur shined like it was newly polished. He was intimidating as a dog. His chest was wide, and his large head was held high. He howled at the moon, and a howl responded. We all scurried over to the window. The full moon lit up the sky. Out in the distance in front of the barn, 12 hounds sat perfectly still in a straight line, with Belle standing at attention like a soldier in front of them. When Jake was himself again, he said, "my dogs are highly intelligent and highly accurate animals. They are now forming an operation of their own led by my girl, Belle."

"Oh, my goodness, Jake! Esther said excitedly.

"Impressive!" James added.

"Very" said John with a smile."

"What about you Miss D? Show us what you got!" Luke said accompanied with "Yea! Come on girl!" from the women. Up until now, I had been afraid of my powers, but watching my friends slip into their essence so effortlessly gave me joy and reassured me that I too could be powerful. So, I closed my eyes. Inside my mind, I saw myself. Long thick black hair, and dark brown skin, but my eyes were all white and glowing. All around my cabin were potted plants and flowers sitting on the wooden floor. Focusing on my power, I heard the window blow open. A powerful breeze floated in carrying small clouds straight from the sky into the cabin. As the clouds circled over the plants scattered across the floor, tiny droplets of water poured from them, watering the soil in each pot. Each plant had its own mini rain cloud hovering above it. I smiled at what I created as claps and cheers filled the room once more.

When it was Lucy's turn, she stood up and exhaled a nervous breath.

"I don't know what to do."

"It's okay, Lucy. Just close your eyes and relax your mind," I encouraged her.

She closed her eyes and stood totally still. Seconds later, her face began to contort into a look of discomfort. Her eyes squeezed tighter although they remained closed. When she opened her eyes, they were completely black, her irises gone. We all looked on, not helping but to be a little bit frightened. She said in a voice that echoed, "The spirit of death is coming to take a wounded soldier home so he can find rest. Don't cry for him. Pray for the journey of his soul to the ancestor's realm."

Lucy's irises returned. No one said a word. In her shy low voice Lucy said, "I want to go check on old man Kojo."

# CHAPTER 15 *MASOZI*

When I left Lesedi's cabin, I was lost. I had no idea where I was going next-in life and in the moment. I walked down that dirt road in a daze, my mind encased in a storm. And then there was whistling. It stopped me right in my tracks. I recognized the tune. When my Baba was happy and drunk, he would sing that very tune. Memories of home flooded in. I spent my whole life hating my home, hating my childhood, and hating my life. Now it was the only thing I thought about; The only thing I missed. I spent so much time in misery, obsessing about the things that I didn't have. I realized now that there was not enough time spent enjoying tunes being whistled, and freedom.

The tune drew me in, and before I knew it, my feet were walking towards elder Kojo who was picking peaches from the tree.

As I approached him, he continued whistling. He plucked a plump peach, inspected it, and threw it to me. I sat down by a nearby tree and bit into the juicy fruit. It was so delicious. I closed my eyes and savored its taste.

"Ya know, when I was a boy in the bush, I climbed fruit trees to the top. That's where the sweetest fruit is. I's old now so Kojo don't climb no more, but why don't you climb on up there and grab a few for an old man?"

I stopped mid-bite and looked at him. I don't think I've ever climbed a tree in my life, but I knew better than to deny the humble request of an elder. So, I stood up, and said "I never climbed a tree before. I had to work as a child."

"You still got breath, boy? Your body and mind still working?"

It wasn't a question, it was a statement. That's all he said, but it was enough. It made me feel, I don't know, inspired maybe? So, I positioned the peach in my mouth, grasping it between my teeth, and jumped up to grab a huge branch with both hands. I pulled myself up with ease. I felt a rush of joy and energy. It pushed me, and I couldn't stop myself. I kept climbing. Soon I was at the top. The view was breathtaking. Rows of manicured vegetation in an array of colors. The sun in the bright blue sky, and the glittering river water that danced beneath it. I perched myself on a branch and resumed eating the peach I carried with my teeth while throwing down gorgeous ripe fruit into the handwoven basket Kojo carried below. When I looked down at him, I was smiling. He took a bite of the peach with the side of his mouth then lifted it up at me. I lifted my peach in return and we both took a bite. From then on, I began sharing a cabin with "old man Kojo" as he called himself. He was nothing like my Baba, but he still reminded me so much of him. He was the Baba I wish I had. He told me stories and spoke in riddles. It was like a game trying to figure out what he wanted me to know. And each lesson seemed to unlock a part of me I didn't know was there.

Kojo spent most of his life as a slave but was still so wise. I felt like a child again around him. After working in the fields, he'd tend to the slave's gardens, handpicking vegetables and pulling weeds. And he cooked and cooked well. He'd recall stories of watching his grandmother cook as a boy, and how he'd burn his mouth stealing spoonfuls of simmering stews. He moved slowly, and his back was hunched but his quick mind made him seem younger than he was. One night over stewed goat he told me how he was stolen from his village at the age of 12. He was the oldest boy with four younger sisters that he hadn't seen since then. In slavery, he had a daughter and son who were both sold away in their teens. He talked about his wife, who died a few years ago, and how much she suffered, how he was glad the spirit of death took her home, and how he prayed to his mother to greet her. I never told Kojo how it came to be that I ended up here. I was too ashamed. For once in my life, I had what felt like the love and direction of a father, and I didn't want to disappoint him. In this short amount of time, he had become more of a parent to me than my own mama or baba ever was. I understand my mama had no choice, but here it was, I was here in her reach, and she hadn't been back to see me since that day in Lesedi's cabin. I became a man with dark secrets I would never speak. To my advantage, I've found speaking less has made me a better listener. My old life is behind me now. In this new life I am a new man; a better man.

Kojo usually rises before the sun. Each morning, I'd find him at the table with his coffee while the roosters called. But this morning, the cabin was quiet. The cool autumn chill settled on the hardwood floor. I made my way to light a fire and roast the beans that would make our coffee. When I approached Kojo, he was still in bed with his eyes closed. Beads of sweat adorned his head like a crown.

"Kojo," I called to him while shaking him softly. He stirred and opened his eyes.

"Old Kojo don't feel too good today. Gonna take my rest."

I looked at him thoroughly now that the light from the fire had illuminated the small space. His brown skin looked yellowish. Even the whites of his eyes seemed a faint shade of egg yolk. His skin was hot to the touch. I poured some water and urged him to drink. I didn't want to leave him there alone, but when he dozed back off into a sleep, he was so peaceful I dared not bother him. I decided I'd ask Lesedi to check in on him today while I was away.

That morning, I had to explain to the overseer that the old man was sick in bed. He laughed and said "old Andre ain't gone be happy to hear about another nigger dying. Guess there might have to be some baby making to balance out the numbers," while eyeing the row of women bent over picking cotton in the rows left of him. I wanted to strangle him. I was already on edge, and it took everything inside of me not to grab his pink throat with my mahogany hands. He must have felt my anger rising, because he moved in close and began speaking in a slower harsher tone. He told me after I finished my chores for the day, that I would begin Kojo's job of picking fruit, nuts, crops, and anything that could be collected and stored on the plantation. Kojo was old and weaker now, so that was all his body allowed him to do. And around here, everybody worked. Elders and children were not exempt.

By the time I returned to the cabin, it was already nightfall. I was sweaty, dirty, and itching because the mosquitoes from the nearby swamp were still lingering around the cabins, even though summer had dwindled and was now over.

When I stepped into the cabin, I was surprised to see Lesedi, Lucy, Esther, Julie, and her daughter Tilly all sitting around Kojo's bed.

"What's this?" I asked as I entered and walked directly to Kojo's bedside. I stood beside it, my eyes glued on Lesedi.

"Yellow fever," she said in a somber tone. "It's going around-the mosquitoes."

Before I could say anything, Kojo said in a strained weak voice "I told Lesedi here don't heal me. Old Kojo is tired, and I'm ready to go on up yonder."

"It is not the time yet, Kojo," I snapped. I didn't mean to, it just came out. Little Tilly got up from where she was sitting between her mama and Lucy and made her way towards me. We all watched her as she walked and put her arms around me. The power of her hug caught me off guard and froze me in place. I hadn't felt the warmth of a hug since- I don't even know when. I just looked down at her, not knowing how to react. She looked up at me with that round face, chubby cheeks, and pigtails dangling and said "we're not just here for grandpa Kojo. We're here for you too. Right mama?" She looked at the beautiful woman who was smiling with watery eyes and nodding.

"Because we are family. Family is the bond you create with the people you love. And we love Kojo, and Kojo loves you, so we love you too," the little girl said with a smile as she looked up at me with the most innocent expression.

The women in the room all had adoration in their eyes. Julie welcomed Tilly back into her lap and pulled her close to her.

Lesedi stood up and moved to the bed. I was still holding Kojo's hand. Lesedi moved hers inside my free hand. Tilly walked up and grabbed her other, and soon we were all holding hands around the bed. Lucy started humming and Esther, Julie and Lesedi joined in. I just stood there, eyes wide and mouth slightly open, hoping I was imagining what I was seeing. The women were humming and Lesedi was chanting in Eleguan. Lucy was translating the words and speaking them aloud. In her native tongue, Lesedi spoke the words "The sacred cycle has spun again. Life reclaimed is life reborn. For your wisdom and sacrifice we thank you elder Kojo. May your journey be peaceful. May we see you on the other side."

Lucy repeated the words in her language. She was holding a beaded necklace in one hand and a carved wooden figure in the other. She rubbed both items with her thumbs.

Her eyes were a complete shade a black. I gasped and stumbled backwards. Lesedi's eyes were white, Esther's blue, Julie's an amber brown, and Tilly's purple. I looked around in horror wondering what was happening. They were still holding hands with each other and Kojo, whom I knew was now dead. His labored breathing was no longer apparent. The room echoed with the sound of Kojo's voice, although his body laid still.

"Masozi. Remember the lion. The Lioness is the hunter, but the Lion protects the pride. You, my son, are a Lion."

And then, for the first time in my life, I cried.

I cried real, heavy, long, sad tears. I fell to the floor heavy under the weight of my sorrow. I felt soft arms encircling me and a warm voice said "it's alright. Let it all out. Ain't gone do you no good to keep it in."

Julie was now sitting on the floor with me, holding my head to her shoulder and cooing me like a baby- another first for me. Lesedi and Julie helped me to a chair before handing me a warm mug filled with a liquid that smelled as sweet as an apple. I drank it without a second thought, and its warmth filled me. I began to fill a surge in my energy. I was mesmerized by it. I could hear the women talking, although now consumed by my own thoughts they seemed a world away.

"We need to discuss how we're gonna handle this situation. Master ain't gone be happy about this, and Wayne's gone try to use that to his advantage."

"What do you suggest we do Esther?" Lucy asked sweetly.

"I suggest we stick with what works. Like what we did for Rachell. We tell master someone else came down with yellow fever too, and that Lesedi nursed them into a full recovery. That might lessen the blow of having to tell the master he lost a slave. Maybe if he thinks we also saved one, we can keep Wayne at bay."

Lesedi agreed saying "That's a great idea Esther."

The women left for the night to inform John of Kojo's passing. John came with a few other men to remove the body. One of them was Jake. He had accompanied the men along with his wife Julie, who was carrying a plate filled with cuts of fried chicken, collard greens, and a cob of corn. The sting of losing Kojo made me oblivious to the fact that all of these supposed slaves had just done Eleguan magic around me. What was life right now? The fact that all of this was even happening. Life was so different from what I'd ever known it to be, or ever thought it could be. It made me feel like I didn't know anything anymore. Not even myself. Things were becoming clearer to me, and that was confusing. Because the things that were becoming clear didn't make sense. These waves of emotions were beginning to overwhelm me. I paced back and forth in an attempt to calm myself.

When that didn't work, I opened up my mouth to yell out a desperate cry of despair. Imagine my surprise when the sound that escaped my mouth was a roar.

# CHAPTER 16 *LESEDI*

The morning after Kojo passed was bright and sunny; the kind of morning that tricks you into believing it's going to be a good day. I was at my altar when a knock sounded at the door. I eased off the floor and walked slowly to open the door. Rachell stood there with bags beneath her eyes.

"Come on in, girl," I said softly, happy to have her company even though I knew whatever brought her here wasn't good. She sat down and dropped her head.

"There's so much happening. Something's going on with Ben, I can feel it. Then Kojo passed... and now Master wants to see you in the house. Lesedi, I'm scared."

I blew out a breath. I felt my heart rate speed up at her last admission but decided to ask, "what's going on with Ben?"

"I don't know. He won't talk to me. He's never been a talking man, but the two of us, we had a bond. Or at least I thought we did. I was treated better, I can admit that, but I shared everything I had with him. But now I think he's starting to resent me."

"Rachell, I'm so sorry. Do you want me to try to talk to him for you? Maybe it's not what you think it is."

"No, thank you but I'm sure it is exactly what I think it is. I think I just needed to say it out loud. I know what I must do." She tried to crack a smile and failed. We hugged and headed off to the house together; Rachell to start the day's work, and me to face whatever awaited me.

We made our way across the field to the huge white structure. The branches of the magnificent willow trees were swaying to the breeze. Master and Zoya were waiting on the porch. Master was dressed in all white and puffing a cigar with a white hat atop his head. Zoya was wearing a brilliant blue gown that seemed to accentuate her bosom. When I approached them, I stopped in my tracks and said nothing. Rachell continued into the house. I stood still waiting to be told what was expected of me today.

"So yellow fever is here is what they're telling me. I hear you saved one life, but the old man died." A puff of smoke escaped his mouth. "Yellow fever is taking over the parish. Upstanding white men are losing money. The Jackson plantation has a damn epidemic. You're going to go over there for a few days and help heal the niggers there.

Robert and I have already settled it and he paid me a good price. I told him I expect him to return you intact. The gods smiled on me that day they hand delivered me a healer slave woman. I'm making a good profit this season." He puffed the cigar again and spat.

"Get what you need and meet John at the stable. You're leaving today."

I opened my mouth to protest but thought better of it. "Yes sir," I replied, trying to disguise the anger rising in my belly. I locked eyes with Rachell who was watching from the doorway. She had been pretending to polish a banister on the grand staircase. She gave me a knowing look. A confident and secure look. Her eyes were saying "don't worry, I got you."

The walk back to the cabin seemed longer today than ever before. I fought the tears that stung my eyes and tried to remind myself I'd be returning soon. What if he sent me all over the parish, renting me from plantation to plantation? All kinds of thoughts were flooding my mind. I was beginning to think about the General's plan a little differently now. Maybe we should burn everything down. No, Lesedi you know better than that was the next thought that followed. When thunder cracked, I became aware of the sudden change in the weather. In my anxiety, the sky had darkened. It was still morning, but storm clouds had completely blocked out the sun. And my hands, they were tingling. I took a deep breath and willed myself to calm down. The clouds parted and the sun was back like it never left.

I walked inside the cabin that had become somewhat of a home to me over the past few months. In the corner was a beautiful wooden trunk that was in the cabin when I arrived. I pulled it to the center of the room and opened it. I packed my other dress, undergarments, my quilt, and my entire store of herbs, and a few yams, and peaches I kept in my stores. I thought about adding the flower to the trunk but decided instead to carry it in my hair, just as my mother had.

A knock again sounded at the door. "Who is it?" I called.

"John," a deep serious voice answered back. I rushed and opened the door. John's face was unreadable as we exchanged good mornings. John spoke calmly as he said "You need to know what to expect. Robert Jackson's plantation ain't like it is here. Just be sure to keep your eyes open and your mouth closed. Stay safe. The general is there, but he is a driver like me, so his loyalty will always be portrayed as to the master. Don't forget that. I'll be checking in on you during my travels."

I couldn't find the words. So instead, I reached out and grabbed his hands with both of mine and held them tight. He returned the squeeze and gave me a nod. He grabbed my trunk and we headed to the mule pulled wagon. Dark clouds followed us the entire way there. It was becoming harder and harder to steady myself.

The first thing I noticed when we arrived was the condition of the slave cabins. They were decrepit moss-covered wood structures with raggedy roofs and hanging wood planks.

The mule came to a stop in front of the big house. There was a white man standing there in a dirty white shirt, overalls, and a straw hat. His long greasy hair hung out around the sides. Where master Rousseau was well dressed and polished, this Robert Jackson looked unkept. Standing beside him was a slightly taller and slimmer white man who seemed to be a younger version of him. John exited the wagon, took his hat to his chest, and gave the master a tiny bow. I exited and stood behind John. I was feeling crippling fear. Flashbacks from the middle passage that I pushed to the back of mind had made a grand arrival and I was struggling to keep my face blank. John did not speak. He handed the white man a note from his pocket. The man took it, read it, and placed it in his shirt pocket.

"Come here girl, let me look at ya," The dirty man spat. I slowly walked forward, keeping my eyes on the ground.

"You'll be staying in Emma's cabin. Emma's going to move into the kitchen until this is all over. She's too valuable to me. I can't afford for her to get sick. I got six niggers here with yellow fever. They're quarantined off in the slave quarters. Until they are all healed don't you or them better leave them quarters, you understand me girl? I ain›t got time for nobody else to get sick."

"Yes sir," I replied with my eyes on the ground trying to control my breathing. When I looked up, I noticed that both men were eyeing me up and down hungrily. I snatched my eyes away and saw the general, known here as "Charles" was now approaching. When Charles arrived, I noticed he was carrying a large iron ring full of keys in the loop of his pants. His master trusted him enough to carry keys? Beside him was an old black woman. She was short and wore a scowl. There was a scar across her right eye. Her hair was covered with a white wrap, and she wore an apron over her dress.

The grim look of everything around here was depressing. There were no gardens outside the cabins. No one talked. Even the crops looked duller. There was no swamp or water around, and very few trees. The slaves here looked soulless. Like shells of the people, they once were.

Emma was quick. She walked at a pace I had to skip to keep up with. As we walked through the wild fields, she stopped and bent down, pulled a knife out of her apron, and chopped the weeds at her feet. She took a cut of one and put it in her mouth. Slowey chewing it before placing the bunch of roots inside her apron. As we walked back to Emma's cabin, all I could think about was how the master and his son eyed me up and down. I had no desire to stay in Emma's cabin alone. The kitchen was its own cabin behind the big house. Kitchens here were made separate from the house to keep the heat from the cooking food and the Louisiana summers from overheating its occupants. And Jackson made it known I'd be left here alone to fend for myself. If anyone tried me today, I'd make it rain heavy hail. At this point I can feel my unstable patience slipping away.

She led me to a dark corner of the slave's quarters before leading me inside a broken-down cabin. The inside was dusty and there was no bed, just a pallet of straw, old fabrics and worn quilts. There was a table and one chair. Overhead there were roots hanging- a tell-tale sign of a healer.

"You and I will split the responsibilities to start, then you'll be on your own. Round here they've been draining blood tryna drip the infection out, but that aint do nothing but speed up death. I'm hoping you come with remedies," she looked at me expectantly.

"Uh, yes mam. I was hoping we could work together and combine our magi-, I mean herbs," I replied.

She looked at me and said "Mmm hmm. Don't expect me to cook for you and feed you. Everybody makes their own way around here. I'll bring you a few rations to get you started for now but then you're on your own."

I nodded and said, "yes, mam."

She quietly studied me for a minute. When I looked in her eyes her scowl had softened into a look of concern, or maybe pity.

"Look, child, I know this is hard. But life is hard. You work and you die. That's it. But you better always keep your head up. Don't let me catch you looking at the floor no more, you hear me?"

She didn't blink and her eyes did not move until I responded. With a sheepish smile I looked at her again and said, "yes, mam." Something about her was so familiar. I just couldn't put my finger on it.

We started right away working on a remedy. Emma shared with me a few of the remedies she used on a regular basis. Tansy tea, catnip, mullein, and sweet gum were among her favorites. There were a few of mine too, although she did school me on some other uses for the herbs that I didn't know about. Like using catnip for babies with colic. We decided to start by creating a tonic of our own special herb blend. Tansy, catnip, mullein, and sweet gum were Emma's contributions. I added sassafras, ginger, elderberry, and silkweed. Emma was easy to talk to. She was hard, she cursed a lot, and was generally just negative in general. But she was also funny, wise and sweet. And although I was slipping into darkness once more, I thanked the ancestors for Miss Emma being a safe place to land.

Emma hung a kettle in the fireplace and lit a fire under it. We added all our ingredients to the kettle and boiled it to a bubbly froth. We then poured the tonic in two large brown necked stone jugs. Emma took one in her arms and motioned for me to grab the other. We walked out of the cabin with the jugs in hand.

"You're gonna see about the three cabins over here, and then the three on the other side. You'll start here," she said as we approached the front door of the cabin next door. I followed closely behind her. We entered the small dark cabin.

On a pallet in the corner lay a brown skin child whose almond brown skin was tinged yellow. His eyes were closed, and his long, lush eyelashes rested on his sweet face. Beads of sweat lingered on his forehead around a head of full dark thick curls. He had to be around the same age as Tilly. One look at him told me this child worked like an adult. He had muscles defined. This poor baby.

"This here is Dillon. He ain't but 11 years old. Master just paid a lot of money for him. Ain't been here but a few weeks. He's the baby of a bred couple. The mama and daddy were both strong as an ox, Master says. Dillon is an investment who he wants you to protect. He's living and working under the blacksmith here. He'll probably be round to check on him. He comes everyday secretly because the master don't want nobody around the sick slaves. But the blacksmith took a liking to the little one. And the boy needs a daddy, so I keep his secret. And I hope you will too."

She looked at me with those unblinking eyes and raised eyebrows.

"Yes, mam, of course. I won't say a word."

"Good. After that you will also have to go see about Rosalie. She's sick and her baby was also ill. We lost the baby yesterday. Rosalie ain›t doing too good. She in the next cabin over. Ima be tending to the house. You just start there, and I'll be round to check on you."

Emma departed and I quickly began tending to the sick child. He was awake, although his yellow eyes were barely open. I walked over to him and kneeled beside him.

"Hi, Dillon. You can call me Miss D. I'm here to take care of you." I said as sweetly as I could manage.

"Hi Miss D," he replied in a strained voice. I looked around and noticed there was no wood for a fire. The tonic in the stone jug was still warm so I decided to give him that first before searching for some wood and returning. After filling up a small, dented tin cup, I knelt beside him again and lifted his body, holding him in my arms like an overgrown baby. I slowly poured the contents of the tin cup into his mouth.

"How is that?" I asked.

"Good," he said, breathing deeply and closing his eyes. I held him in my arms until I knew he was sleeping- the results of the herbs and roots going to work in his body. Flashbacks of Abeena and her young son jumping into the ocean threatened my ability to keep my composure. I closed my eyes and took a few deep breaths myself before laying Dillon back down and exiting the cabin.

The cool air was a welcome refreshment, but the air soon reminded me this was no place to be refreshed. Carrying my stone jug, I entered the cabin that Emma told me was Rosalie's. Inside was a small frail light skinned woman with long wavy black hair. Her eyes were sunken, and her skin had the same yellow tinge I was now accustomed to seeing.

"Who is you?!" she spat. She never turned her head to face me.

"I'm here to take care of you, Miss Rosalie. My name is Lesedi."

She scoffed. "And I don't have no say so over if I live or die huh? Cause ima slave? She paused, and I stood there silent. She gave a bitter laugh before turning to face me with a look on her face that was truly frightening.

"What I got to live for? My baby girl is dead!" She was screaming now, and her face was red, before breaking into a violent cough. She held a cloth to her mouth that had been stained with specks of blood.

"Get out! I don't want no medicine, I just want to die right here. And I don't care if they come and whip me again. I want them to! I just want to die!"

She cried and cried and cried. Uncontrollable sobs. I just stood there. I had no idea what to say, or how to console her. Her darkness had consumed her. I could easily see nothing I could say would remedy the loss of her baby girl. So, I said "okay. If that is what you wish, I will respect that. I will tell them we medicated you, but you died of grief." She just looked at me and blinked. I continued.

"I know it doesn't seem like it now. But there is life on the other side of pain. If you would be brave enough to keep living, it might surprise you what you're capable of."

She didn't respond. She looked away from me. Silent tears now streaking her face.

"Just think about what I said, and I'll come back and check on you tonight."

She didn't respond but I knew my words were not lost on her.

I'm starting to notice that the answers that I seek for myself sometimes come in the form of advice I give to others. I understand Rosalie's pain. Her pain is my pain in many ways. And even though it was easy for me to tell her there was life on the other side of pain, I honestly wasn't sure if that life was a life worth living. But what would be the alternative? Living and dying as a slave? I owed it to myself and my ancestors to keep living. And so did Rosalie. And I believed in due time she'd see that too.

After distributing the herbal tonic Emma and I created amongst the ill slaves, I decided to go back to Dillon's cabin. I wanted to keep an eye on the child, and I admittedly didn't want to be alone. Dillon was still asleep when I returned. Emma stopped by to drop off a few scraps of bread left over from dinner in the big house. She apologized and said it was all she could sneak out. I thanked her and watched her leave to spend her night in the kitchen. I went back to check on Rosalie who this time did not refuse my tonic. It was cold now, but it would work all the same. On my way back to Dillon's cabin I grabbed a few branches for a fire. I wondered what the boy had been eating. I wish I would have thought to bring the peaches and yams stored in my trunk. I made a mental note to stop by Emma's empty cabin after dropping off the wood. I reached down to grab a thick piece of fallen bark for the fire when I saw the general approaching me on horseback. He looked down at me with dark cold eyes and spoke.

"Master wants a report on the sick slaves. Wants to make sure he's getting his money's worth out of you."

"Well, um, all their fevers have broken thanks to the tonic Emma, and I mixed. I think with some rest they should recover in a few days' time."

"Show me," he said blankly. So, I gestured for him to follow me inside Dillon's cabin. He was still sleeping peacefully, his skin looking a little browner than before. Charles walked up to him and placed a hand to his forehead. Nodding his approval.

"So, she really is a healer," he said condescendingly with a smirk on his face. Without a look back he walked out the cabin door. That last remark sparked the lighting in my fingers. Something about this Charles was off to me. It bothered me that I couldn't understand him. I remember John's words about the general being perceived to be a loyal driver, but still. All the events of the day had me a little fired up, honestly. I'm over this slave life. Living in squalor with no control over my own decisions. I have the power to burn this place down right now if I so choose but what would it solve? It wouldn't bring mama back or bring me any closer to finding baba and returning home.

I was starting the fire and brewing in frustration. I threw the wood into the fireplace before zapping it with lighting. I all but threw the kettle on top of it. My frustration had slowly burned into anger, and by the time I had the fire going, I was steaming. When the cabin door creaked open, I snapped my head to it. If it was Charles again with something smart to say, I swore to the skies I would electrocute him.

Right there in front of me was a sight that made my heart stop. I'd recognize that face in any realm. I felt like I was being transported back to a time so far gone now. He was dirty from working in the forge, just like he used to be back home. Bearded and black was my love, Ukize. Glistening in the orange setting sun like dark ripe fruit on a vine. I was lost. I couldn't find any words. All I could do was stare in disbelief. He stared back at me with his eyes and mouth wide open. I stood up and placed my hands over my mouth, shaking my head and now crying. Ukize blinked a few times as if he couldn't believe his eyes. Then he closed the door and locked it hurriedly, and I ran to him. He pulled me in his arms and squeezed me. Both of us with tears flowing uncontrollably.

"Lesedi. Lesedi. I cannot believe it. How can it be?" His deep voice cracked as he bellowed the words. I just cried.

Ukize placed both hands on each of my cheeks and looked down into my wet eyes. And then he kissed me. We melted into one another. A kiss so slow and deep and full of passion; a kiss that held all the words we could not say; a kiss that symbolized the gratitude for the refuge our love provided. We pulled back and stared at each other again just to make sure it was real. I wrapped my arms around Ukize's waist and laid my head on his hard chest. He wrapped me tightly and nestled his head into my soft hair.

Quietly, he whispered "I knew it. I knew you would survive. My girl is stronger than them all." His voice carried a tone of pride. I felt as though my heart was going to burst. Finally, I said "We should sit and have a meal." He looked at me and smiled. Then he kissed my forehead and said "Come, I have a few things stored."

# CHAPTER 17 *UKIZE*

I am a man. I was raised by real men. Warriors, kings, hunters, men of God. My right of passage was five days in the bush with only my spear. I returned without a scratch. But this... this evil of slavery will break even the strongest man. Many nights I lie awake wondering why. But I am an Eleguan man. I get weak but I refuse to break. More than that, I refuse to be broken by the likes of these cowards with superior weaponry. I teach Dillon the ways of the Eleguan man, ensuring that he too will survive. Faced one on one with the enslavers, I am the stronger man, and I know that. So, I keep my mind and body healthy. I pray every day facing East. Facing home. And I remember; I remember where I came from; I remember my name; I remember my love. *Lesedi.* Her smile always made me feel better. My baba was no-nonsense. He was strict but attentive. He taught me real men provide and protect. There is no time for games or laughs. Life is serious business, and as men, we must be serious about our business. But Lesedi was free. She smiled and laughed and dreamed. She'd hold my rough hands in her smaller, softer ones and lock our fingers together while she rested her head on my shoulder. Her hair always smelled like flowers. Her love for me was always warm, devoted, faithful, and true. I had planned to propose to her the night of the Feast of the Full Moon, but that night and every night since then has been stolen from me. I knew I would see her again. My girl is strong. I've seen her with a staff. Watching her work is one of my favorite pastimes. She's not just a pretty-faced princess, she's the future chief and lethal with a staff. She could bring the biggest man to his knees. That's what I love about her, her fire. Yes, she's sweet, warm, and kind, but she is also fierce, fiery, and impossibly persistent. She hated being told she could not do something, so she decided she could do everything. She learned the roles of the men and the women, stating it was her duty as future chief, and outperformed even the highest ranked soldiers. Then she'd go back to daydreaming and picking flowers. I was in love from the first day she smiled at me. But apart from that is the fact my mind wouldn't let me believe otherwise. I had to believe she kept going, it was the only thing that kept me going.

I walked into the cabin that evening exhausted. I was told by Emma earlier that day Master rented a healer woman from the Frenchman's plantation. Never once did I imagine it would be her. My girl. I dropped to my knees and thanked God the moment I saw her. And I cried. For the first time in forever. I unleashed an ocean of tears that she bathed in. She wouldn't let me go. Her arms locked around my body and her forehead nestled in my neck. We stayed that way for I don't know how long. Time stood still.

I didn't want to leave the cabin for anything, not even for food. Now the Lesedi was in my presence, I'd make sure it stayed that way for as long as time would allow. From a high shelf, I pulled out a small worn basket. Inside were wild greens, wild mushrooms, and a few nuts. Lesedi looked at the contents and smiled.

"A man that can survive in the bush can survive anywhere," she teased. It was a saying between us Eleguan men. Surely, she could tell by my food selection I'd been surviving off my foraging skills. She was observant like that, plus she possessed the same skills.

"Hold on. I'll be right back," Lesedi said with a smile.

I felt the sting of tears in my eyes and fought hard to hold them back. It was like she never left. We were here in the middle of slavery, but it seemed as if it was only us two, just like it had always been. She took off running. A few minutes later, she returned holding three yams and three peaches. She showed me the bread Emma dropped off, and then she started cooking. When she asked if I had a knife, I pulled one from the holder on my waist; a blade I forged myself. I was quite proud of it, so I kept it hidden. It was small and deadly like the fangs of a panther. She looked beautiful chopping yams into large chunks with the knife I made. It fit perfectly in her hands. I sat on the floor up against the wall with my long legs out in front of me. Dillon had awakened by this time. The two of us listened silently with love and adoration as Lesedi went on and on about the friends she'd made, and how happy she was that Sky Mother has brought us all together today, and how that was proof that there is real life after pain. And not only that, but also there can be love in that life. I smiled the whole time. My cheeks were starting to hurt. I smiled more today in the short time I spent reunited with my girl than I had since we were captured months ago. Her spirit remained bright no matter what. After all this, her words were of happiness and gratefulness. A broken woman who had assembled the puzzle of herself and carried on, refusing to be anything less than whole.

Her hips swayed as she checked on Dillon and stirred the pot of wild greens, mushrooms, nuts, and yams. I watched her intently as she threw a few of her herbs in there too. It smelled like heaven. And when she filled our bowls, it tasted even better.

Lesedi attended to Dillon like a mother would a child, and it made me love her even more. Dillon seemed to have taken to her too because he was smiling. The boy smiled just about as much as I did, which was basically never. But not tonight. My girl was here and there was nothing but a smile on both of our faces. I decided right then and there I was done being a slave. Whatever I had to do to leave here with my girl, we would do it. We could run to the swamps. My girl was tough, so I knew she could survive there. And I'd been teaching Dillon discreetly how to do the same. He would come with us too soon as he was healed.

After dinner and conversation, Dillon drifted back off into sleep. I was so happy to see the progress his health had made. He'd be himself again in no time under her care.

Lesedi and I were sitting on the floor up against the wall holding hands and watching Dillon sleep. I rested my chin in her soft curls, inhaling her scent. She looked up at me and softly asked "What's his story?"

"He doesn't talk much about it, but from what I heard he was born on a breeding plantation in Georgia. He is the son of the strongest woman and man. He came at a hefty price. When I got here, I found work right away working iron. Master's been raving about all the money in metal work there is now, so when the boy came, he was sent to apprentice under me. I noticed his strength right away, but he's still a child. And I don't know, I guess it broke my heart a little. I saw myself in him you know, but at least I had my mama and baba. Who does he have?"

"He has you," she replied sweetly.

"And you?"

"Yes, and me too. You both do."

I looked around the cabin. Dillon was sleeping peacefully, and the fire was slowly dying. In a hushed tone, I looked at her seriously and said "run away with me, Lesedi. Soon as Dillon has his strength, let's leave this place. I know a man living in the swamp colony. We could stay there for a time until we figured out where to go next. Just say yes."

She looked at me with loving eyes and said, "I have so much to tell you." She slowly recalled the details of her journey, starting with the innocence that was taken from her aboard the slave ship. She spoke of the flower she carried, and all the spiritual people Sky Mother placed in her life since leaving Elegua that have guided her to this moment. When she got to her meeting with Miss Dupont, her face turned serious. She told me how Miss DuPont told her and Charles (who was the insurrection leader which was completely shocking to me. judging by the way he carried on around here) that she was chosen to lead us all to freedom, and how he scoffed at her. And that she had restored the magic of a few, and she would restore mine next. I sat there processing this wealth of information she laid upon me. Sky Mother was still with us indeed. And Lesedi carried the lotus of the first mother.

I took a deep breath, slowly processing all of what I'd just been told.

"My love, there's something that you should know."

She looked at me with wide eyes. I could practically see the panic rushing in. I exhaled and said "Your Baba, he's here. And so is Kendi." She gasped and covered her mouth.

I hung my head and said "They're different now, you should know that."

"Different how?" she questioned. I thought for a minute and answered.

"They're broken. This place-it breaks slaves. The master literally calls himself the slave breaker. Kendi and I arrived here at the same time, but your baba was brought here from a neighboring plantation. They said he had been causing too much ruckus, getting the slaves all riled up with talk of rebellion. He even ran away, but didn't get far before the dogs were on him. When the dogs found him, they didn't bite. They just stared at Rasaq, and him back at them. It drove the masters crazy that the dogs wouldn't attack. After that, they tortured him; beat him and placed him in a man-made jail. A steel box with metal spikes protruding from the walls. But every time he'd heal, he'd go back to his anti-slavery carrying on, so they keep beating him and putting him back in that steel box. He's still in there now, he's been there for about a week."

Lesedi didn't respond. Tears streaked her cheeks as her frown turned into a snarl.

"Will you take me to him?" she asked firmly.

"Yes," I replied without a second thought. I had been sneaking him my rations and knew the best way to go unseen. The panther blood was still in me. I still knew how to be sleek and cling to the shadows. She reached into her braids and pulled out the sacred glowing lotus. I stared at it, in awe of its beauty. Even with a few missing petals.

With the kettle now void of our wild greens and mushroom stew, Lesedi filled it with water and dropped in a single petal. She spoke aloud to herself in Eleguan as she worked, reminding me of the older women back home who would do the same while working busily in the kitchen.

"And what of Kendi?" she asked blankly while waving her hand over the kettle and evoking some type of misty purple vapor. Dillon stirred in his sleep but did not awaken.

"Well, Kendi is... let's just say angry."

"Join the club," Lesedi said agreeingly.

I looked at her anxiously. "It's not good, my love. You'll see what I mean."

She didn›t respond. Instead, she continued to move busily in silence. She then poured the steaming purple liquid into the dented tin cup and handed it to me. I looked at the contents and closed my eyes. I began to pray out loud.

"Thank you, Sky Mother, for your blessings. I pray you guide me, protect me, and equip me to fulfill your purpose for my life. Ase."

"Ase'," Lesedi repeated.

I drank it down quickly and immediately felt its warmth. A purple glow began radiating all around me. Dillon awakened with a look of wonder on his face. Before he could ask a question, Lesedi was pushing the same dented cup in his hands and urging him to drink. The same purple glow was now surrounding Dillon. The yellow in his eyes was turning darker into a midnight shade of gold. They had taken on a cat-like shape; slanted with the gleam of an obsidian glow. The cub of a big cat stood before me looking happy and playful.

I looked at Lesedi, and she was smiling.

"Such a handsome panther you've always been, and it looks like now that there are two handsome panthers."

I could feel the fire in my veins. My catlike senses reunited with my being. I was home again in my body. And it was on now.

With my power now restored I felt untouchable. Dillon spoke more than I ever heard him speak this whole time we've been together. He asked Lesedi and me what seemed like a million questions about our homeland and magic. He was so excited and spoke so long that Lesedi brewed up some chamomile and feverfew to put him back to sleep. All traces of yellow fever were now gone. With Dillon sleeping, and the black of night comfortably resting in the sky, Lesedi and I decided it was the perfect time to go see her baba. As we headed towards the door, I smoothly transformed into my panther form.

"You're going out as a panther?" Lesedi asked shockingly.

"Yes, why not?" I replied coolly with a grin. She rolled her eyes and smiled.

"Ok, I'll cover you," She poured the remaining contents of the lotus tonic into a small flask, and we headed out. As we quietly stepped out into the night, Lesedi's eyes turned white. Soon a dense fog was all around us. It was impossible to see, but my cat eyes guided me effortlessly. I led her to the jail. When we approached it, Lesedi waved her hands, and the fog dissipated into a surrounding circle that encased us around the jail. The circular mist gave only us a line of sight into the jail and prevented us from being seen by anyone that may have been wandering in the night. I walked to the cage slowly with cat-like precision to where Lesedi's baba, Rasaq, was being caged. When he saw me approaching, he did not cower. He eyed me curiously, inclining his head to get a better look. He was bearded and bloody, but his eyes held a terrifying ferocity. I sat by his cage for a moment to see if he would figure it out. And when a grin spread across his tired face, I knew he'd put it all together. His eyes widened with delight.

"How?!" he asked in an excited whisper. Out of the fog stepped Lesedi. Rasaq let out a groan. Silent crocodile tears rained from his dark eyes. Lesedi sat outside the cage and cried too. The protruding spikes inside prevented them from getting any closer.

"What have they done to you, Baba?" The inquiry was barely above a whisper.

"This is nothing," he said in a jagged voice. "I will heal. They're trying to break me, but I refuse to die. Where is your mama, did she come here with you?"

Lesedi hung her head. "Mama is with the ancestors. Her, Abeena, and her boy led an attack on the slave ship before succumbing to the ocean. It was a distraction so mama could give me this."

With her head still hung, Lesedi parted her hair with her hands to reveal the flower hiding inside. Rasaq's silently crying eyes recognized the flower at once. The look in his eyes harbored a deep sadness, but he looked at his daughter with pride.

191

"Chief Lesedi. The new Eleguan queen. May the honorable and beautiful Chief Lyabo rest forever on her throne with the ancestors. Don't worry my love, I will protect our daughter with my life." His words were whispers, but they were strong and defined. He spoke as if we were inside the royal court back home in the sacred center.

"You were chosen by God, my daughter. I always knew you were meant to do great things. And here you are. You survived."

"I found my power, Baba," Lesedi said through a slight smile and tears as she sat on her knees peering in at her beloved father.

"I see my daughter, and what a fine power it is. This fog is wonderous,»he said musically.

"Here, drink this," Lesedi said as she rolled the flask through the bars. It hit the side of Rasaq's barefoot. He reached down to pick it up and was cut by a metal spike. A thin slit began to bleed. On his arms and legs were remnants of scars and open cuts. He'd been taking a beating for a while now, but his Eleguan strength shone through. Ignoring the new cut completely, Rasaq drank greedily. When the purple glow made its appearance, the wounds and abrasions on Rasaq's arms and legs disappeared and were replaced with scales. The cage was too small and dangerous for him to transform into his true animal form, so he sat there embodying a terrifying cross between a crocodile and a husky man. His skin, now a scaly greenish brown, when he smiled it was the snarl of a hungry gator.

"Welcome back Rasaq, the most ferocious croc. I hear there's a few swamps nearby," I said with a grin, now in my human form. He smiled back triumphantly.

"Baba, we have a plan. It requires you to behave, but only for the time being so you can be released from this cage," Lesedi said seriously.

"Once we are reunited, I will give you full details of the plan. For now, rest up, and behave. You can't run until you're released."

He nodded his agreement, and we all shared a loving knowing look between us. Silently solidifying our reunion, and impeding rebellion.

As Lesedi and I walked back to the cabin through the dense fog, my mind was racing with thoughts of ways we could all escape together as a family. Seeing the sacred lotus in Lesedi's hair changed everything. True Eleguans understand the strength of its powers. It has survived many generations because it endures all. The carrier utilizes its power, and when it is passed on, the new barrier harnesses the power of each great barrier that came before her. And now, my panther power has been restored. At home, Rasaq could shift into many animals. Not every man has his gift of power. Today Sky Mother made him a croc. It was a sign that we should head to the swamps, I knew it was.

"Lesedi, what do you know of the swamps nearby?"

"Well... I had to cross through one on my way to the Rousseau plantation. It's close to the slave quarters, but the waters are so muddy and murky, it's impossible to cross without being seen. I came through in the dark of morning right before sunrise, but the entire time I was wading through I felt as if I was being watched. Then once I got on the plantation, I started to hear whispers of the people living in the trees within the swamps, but that's all I know."

"There are rumors here as well. It seems your friend, the lady Miss Dupont is very popular, because the slaves here are also banned from seeing her. That is why the master here called for you. According to Emma, Miss DuPont helped the former blacksmith, a man named Octave escape. Everyone knew Octave was sweet on a medicine woman. I think her name was Franny. And it seems that both Franny and Octave disappeared from their plantation at the same time. The slaveholders just assumed Miss DuPont was involved because she was the only real resource the slaves had access to. Emma says they're correct, but they could never prove it. They can't get close to her even though they've tried. Emma says it's because her magic is too strong," Lesedi stared back with wide eyes.

"I've heard many whispers of Franny and her escape, but this is my first time hearing of Octave."

"Yes, the whispers are he runs the maroon island along with Franny, and he offers asylum to any slave that escapes and pledges their loyalty to his band of Marauder warriors." I watched her roll over my words in contemplation.

"I pledge that we escape into the swamps and join the marauders. All of us. Me, you, Rasaq, Dillon and Kendi too if she so wishes." We stopped walking. The night sky shone bright above us. My attention was suddenly snatched away by the tingling of my senses. I quickly turned my body and felt my eyes and ears tap into their panther sense of awareness.

"Ukize what's wrong?" Lesedi whispered but I did not respond. Instead, I pointed and said, "get down low and clear a line of sight for your eyes only." She laid low on the ground and did just that. Focusing her eyes, she quietly gasped. In front of us was the slave driver Charles, being welcomed into a cabin with a longing kiss from Kendi. She pulled him inside by his collar and slammed the door shut. Lesedi stood up and said nothing. Her eyes were cold. Her face was unreadable. In her face were traces of what looked like sadness, and maybe regret, but also confusion.

"Come, my queen," I said, grabbing her hand. She smiled back sweetly. Quietly we continued our trek.

When we stepped inside the empty cabin the dying fire in the grate was humming in a deep orange glaze. I added a few logs and led Lesedi to my small pallet of quilts in the back shadows where I'd been sleeping. I made myself as comfortable as I could on the hard cold floor. She came and nestled down in front of me. I wrapped my arms around her waist and took in a deep breath, more comfortable on this bed of straw than I've ever been.

"I think you, baba, and Dillon should sneak into the swamps and wait for me there," she whispered.

"That way, we can be close to one another. I can't abandon those I left behind at the Rousseau plantation. We all deserve to be free."

"What do you have in mind?"

"There is talk that if we go west or north, we can be free. My vote is for west, under the protection of the Spanish, we can live free and not have to worry about the enslavers. We won't have to look over our shoulders, and we can create a new Elegua. The swamps are too close to slavery for us to ever be truly free there for a long term. I don't wish to live the rest of my life fighting, and I also don't want to live the rest of my life without you," She turned around to face me.

"I won't leave here without you, Kize. Escape to the swamps and wait for me there. Please."

"Yes. Lesedi of course." It wasn't even a question. Whatever she wanted me to do, I'd do it without a second thought. I know her heart, and I trust her fully. And I know she knows she's safe with me. "I don't wish to be without you another day," I whispered. "At least in the swamp I'm close enough to turn panther and come to you." She smiled at me, and I returned her smile. I kissed her deeply. We stayed that way for a long while before parting to breathe and take measure of the growing heat between us.

"How soon do you wish to leave here?"

"The day you leave this place, is the day I leave too. Dillon and Rasaq as well," I replied.

"I need to talk to Charles alone. Do you think that can be arranged?" I eyed her curiously.

"Lesedi, I don't like this Charles man. I don't know if he can be trusted."

"I share your concerns. But this can't wait. Kize, he carries keys. If he's not on our side, it›s best we find out now."

"I'll mention it to Emma. She can set it up."

"Okay. Thank you Kize."

"Anything for you, my queen." She turned her back to me again and backed her body into mine. I held her tighter. With my face in her neck, I made my way through the hair resting on her nape and kissed it slowly and repeatedly. When I felt her breath deepen and the easy rhythm of her breathy light snore, I knew she was sleeping. I too closed my eyes and slept peacefully for the first time in many many moons.

# CHAPTER 18 *KENDI*

"Charles, can't you stay with me, just for tonight? You always rush off, and I understand why, but I just wish I could have more time with you."

"You know why I can't stay, Kendi. I don't want to keep talking about this. You said you understood."

"I do, it's just... I don't know. I don't like being alone in the dark."

"I told you to make some friends around here, talk to the other women. Sitting around moping won't solve anything."

I hung my head. His words stung, but it was an easy sting compared to the wounds I've accumulated through life. My life has never been easy. Ruled over by an angry baba, forced to marry a man twice my age then sold into slavery when I wouldn't abide him. My innocence was stolen from him first, and then again by a blue-eyed demon who roped my neck and used me like his pet. The nausea of sea voyage mixed with the nausea of childbearing. When I arrived on this plantation, I was six months pregnant by my calculation. The child of the man who sold me. When I entered the slave vessel, I was already dead inside. I remember seeing Lesedi. Her wide and innocent eyes called for me. My oldest friend, my sister. I felt her pain and pity for me. And for some reason I hated her for it. Her life was always so easy. She had family and community and freedom. She got to learn things, and waste time. I loved her then because she loved me. She said we were two sides of the same coin. She had magic and grace and status. But she never saved me, she never came for me. She took my stories of pain and marveled over them as if my plight fascinated her. And the admiration I once felt for her turned into resentment, and then hate. When I saw her eyes that day on the slave ship, they pleaded with me, but I only wished we could trade places; that somehow it would be her this time to feel the sharp pain of life's dagger, and not me on the other end of the blade for once.

And then one night, in my seventh month alone in my cabin I squatted over a stack of hay and delivered a dead baby. The one mercy Sky Mother showed me. I went into the woods to bury my demons, and when I turned around, he was there. Tall and golden skinned, he kneeled down in the dirt and wiped my tears. He said warriors don't cry as he gently held my gaze. He carried me back to my cabin, laid me down, and left. One single act sealed my devotion to him. He was a tortured soul, but he was beautiful. His eyes held deep passion. And despite his inability to love me fully, I knew he only had eyes for me, and that was more than enough.

Each night, he'd sneak into my cabin and bless me with sweet hot passion. His eyes blazed with fire. When his thick pink lips engulfed mine, he took me hungrily. His hands slow and deliberate, his pace forceful and strong. I spent my days picking cotton and my nights riding orgasms. He told me his secrets in the darkness of night, and I told him mine. Forever a militant man, he'd speak of burning desires of freedom, and revenge. His need for retaliation consumed him daily, but he wore an impenetrable mask. Only I could see the real desire behind his eyes. I traced his scars with my fingers as he lay bare and sweaty beside me. Silently, I'd drift away, unknowingly sleeping until I felt the shift of his weight in the night and heard the slow creek of the door. And every morning when I opened my eyes, he was gone.

This morning was no different.

I woke up alone and headed to the fields. He was already

dressed atop his stallion circling the working slaves, playing his position. The slaves hated him. They whispered names like uppity and house nigga. And I hated them for it. I had no desire to make nice with a bunch of judgmental slaves. They didn't understand him, but I did. He seemed unaffected by it. He never smiled or conversed unless he was talking to Emma. I hated her too. Everybody loved Miss Emma. Maybe because she was old, she had more leeway than the rest of us. But that's not why I hated her. I hated her because she was the only person who made Charles smile. He was a warrior. He never smiled. But when Miss Emma appeared, he grinned like a child. She was a distraction.

As I picked the cotton off the needle-like stems, I watched her approach him out of the corner of my eye. She beckoned for him to reach down and hug her, and he abided with a smile. My blood boiled. Watching her blatantly now I saw the shadow of a whisper placed in his ear. He gave a quick terse nod, and she quickly hurried off. When I turned to resume my picking, I found myself being analyzed intently by the master's son who was watching from a distance on the steps of the big house. I lowered my head, but I felt his gaze burning me.

The day went on as usual. That night, I received my rations and returned to my cabin to wait for Charles. I waited and waited, but he never came. Wide awake, curious, and a little angry, I left out into the dark of night headed to his cabin. There was no light or sign of occupancy. As I glanced down the row of cabins in the moonlight, there was only one illuminating light. I slowly and carefully made the journey. Crouching low below the window, I closed my eyes and listened. This was Emma's cabin so I knew this was the only other place Charles could be. When I peeked into the window, my heart stopped. Lesedi. Here with my Charles. How dared she? They spoke directly, and I watched furiously. I heard what sounded like leaves crunching but ignored it. A breath later, I turned around and screamed after being confronted by what looked like a terrifying black panther. The door to Emma's cabin swung open and Charles stood there radiating his anger.

"Kendi," Lesedi whispered. I ignored her. I glanced back again, and the panther was gone. Charles silently and forcefully grabbed me by my arm and all,.but dragged me into the cabin.

"Have you been following me?" he whispered angrily.

"Why are you here alone, with her?" I asked, disgust dripping from my voice.

"Kendi," Lesedi started.

"Don't 'Kendi' me!" I snapped. "Why are you even here? Don't you have magic?" I studied her curiously. She stood there silently with saddest eyes I've ever seen.

Don't tell me you lost it," I said with sarcastic amusement. She looked down with closed eyes, and I laughed. Charles looked between us both with an unreadable expression. He turned to Lesedi and said, "we'll finish this later." Then he turned to me and in a firm voice said, "let's go." As we descended from the cabin Lesedi stood there unmoving looking as if she had seen a ghost.

When we entered my cabin, Charles unleashed his fury.

"Are you crazy? You could have been seen! Everything I've built could all be compromised because you want to play the role of the jealous mistress! This is business! If you can't fulfill your role, you will be replaced!" he screamed. His golden skin was red. Replaced. He said he could replace me. It was never clearer to me than it was in that moment that the nature of men is all the same. They can't be trusted. And I decided I would no longer play by the rules of men. It was finally time for them to learn how to play by mine.

Hurt by his words I said back in a low snakelike voice "If you try it, I will destroy you. I know your secrets, Charles, and I will tell them. You won't leave this plantation without me. I'll make sure of it."

He looked at me with surprise, but quickly caught himself and slipped back under his mask, but this time, I couldn't read him. I was foolish to trust him, he was a man just like the rest of them. And I know men to be arrogant and easily distracted. But I loved Charles, and he was going to be mine, whether he knows it now or not. And if Lesedi, Emma or anybody else got in the way of that, I'd remove them from the picture. Secretly, I'd looked forward to Charles' rebellion, not just for freedom, but because life had made me blood thirsty. I knew Sky Mother killed my baby because she knew if she didn't, I would. But being denied that relief, the shaking anger inside of me still longed to kill what all has been killing me. And if they took Charles from me, I'd start with them.

There was no lovemaking that night. Charles disappeared back into the darkness of the night, and I back into the darkness of my mind. What was Lesedi doing here? I racked my brain trying to solve the puzzle, and then remembered Rasaq and Ukize both were here as well. That is undoubtedly why she came. And that means, the panther I saw tonight was Ukize! Fireworks went off and I sat straight up. She hadn't lost her magic. She still had it. And she gave it to Ukize. Did she give it to Charles too? I've always wanted her magic for my own, and now I finally had the opportunity. I knew all Lesedi's secrets too, and if the magic was here, that meant she had the flower.

# CHAPTER 19 *LESEDI*

I sat outside that morning before sunrise on Emma's steps alone. I closed my eyes and let the cool morning breeze flow over my being. The crisp bite of it was so refreshing. I dreamed of the day I was free. They trapped my body, but they couldn't trap my mind. I won't let them. Once upon a time all I did was dream. I believed there was so much more for me to discover. I make it a point to keep dreaming even though reality is bleak. In my dreams, I'd have a home of my own with a grand porch. All my loved ones would live nearby. I'd sit outside each morning and greet the day. I'd take time talking to Sky Mother and drinking peppermint tea. I'd have sons and daughters of my own that I'd teach all the ways I've learned. Despite my plight, I am grateful for what life has made me. I can admit now that I was naive to the true evils of the world. Evils Kendi knew all about. I feel so foolish now thinking about it. I lived life in color once, but when I was captured, life seemed very black and white. But as I continue on, I find myself in a gray area where two things are happening at once. I am exhibiting great pain but also great strength. I cannot pretend to know what Sky Mother has in store for me, or why she brought me here. I don't even know why she saw me fit. But, at least now, I know that in times of great pain I am evolving. I was always a princess, but now I am a warrior. I move discreetly in the shadows, planting my own seeds of magic. I know nothing worth having will come easy. There is no such thing as a quick fix. The foundation must be laid brick by brick. And I see now that the price of happiness is pain. Even if I fail, I will die as a warrior. I will not die on my knees. I will die with my sphere and my lotus in hand, in head, and in heart. And I shall live forever with my foremothers. And God help whoever tortures those I leave behind, for once I am with the ancestors, I shall haunt them and their descendants with reminders of the Magic we've planted in these lands that we've toiled in, bled in, and died in.

I'm in desperate need of prayer. I need to pray and to be prayed for, because at this point, I can't even begin to comprehend what is happening. All this just seems like a never-ending bad dream. The highs of being reunited with loved ones and the sobering realization of why we got separated in the first place. This time last year, I was skipping rocks in the river. Now I'm on my second plantation. My thoughts are interrupted by the bushy haired silhouette headed my way through the damp morning fog. Her bare feet are wet with the dew from the grass. Kendi.

I stand to greet her and realize as she approaches her eyes harness a darkness I've never seen. I open the door and motion for her to come in. As she steps over the threshold, she looks me up and down.

"So. You have the flower huh? Brought it here to save your beloved Ukize? Or was it for your good and noble Baba?" Kendi was straight to the point. Jealousy dripped off her every word. No reunion, no exchange of love or pleasantries. Just business.

"Kendi, I'm sorry. I'm so sorry. If I could go back and change things, you have to know- "

"Save it. I didn't come here for that. I want the magic. You owe me and-"

"Okay."

"Okay?"

"Yes, okay. You're right. I owe you so much. I love you and I have a plan."

She holds a hand up and stops me mid-sentence.

"I'm not leaving with you. You have Ukize, and now I have Charles."

"Kendi..."

"Lesedi, don't! Don't you dare try to ruin my happiness. He may not be romantic and gallant like Ukize, but he loves me!"

Her eyes were pleading now. Anger and hurt spilling from her being and threatening to leak from her eyes but she doesn't let a tear fall. And I break. This scene of reuniting with my sister is not how it's supposed to be. It's supposed to be a time of happiness, but instead it's so tragic and it's breaking my heart.

"I know you hate me, but I love you. I'm so sorry that I wasn't there for you. I'm so sorry that my naivety stopped me from seeing that you were hurting. I wasn't there for you, I couldn't save you then, and I'm sorry. I will do this for you now because you deserve this. We all deserve happiness, Ken," I look into her eyes looking for a glimpse of the girl I used to know. I don't see her.

"Ukize loves you, you know that? When we first got here, he tried to be my protector out of some misguided loyalty to you. I told him straight away he was wasting his time, because I didn't care whether you lived or died. After that he wouldn't even look at me. He was so angry." She let out a cold chuckle.

"You are lucky. It seems you are still spoiled even here." She paused and looked at the ground. A flash of sadness briefly replaced the look of malice that lined her brow.

"You and I will never be friends again; you should know that."

The words stung with a finality that made my stomach hurt. I knew it, but I wasn't ready to accept it.

"But we'll always be sisters," I whispered in reply.

She didn't say anything. She looked at me expressionless. Feeling the sting of hot tears rolling down my face, I turned away and said "Sit. Let me get it ready."

She sat down without a word, and I headed towards the back where I kept things hidden. My foot hit the flask left over from our meeting with baba last night. When I picked it up, I realized there was still a corner of contents left in the bottle. My initial thought was to boil a new batch, but something inside of me, now seeing the flask, decided against it. I picked it up and handed it to her.

"This is what I gave Baba last night. You are welcome to it," she snatched it from my hands and drank it down greedily. I knew there wasn't much there, so I didn't take long. While she gulped, I whispered a prayer to the mothers, asking that they help Kendi find her way. The contents were much less than I was accustomed to giving, but she seemed to be pleased. There was no purple glow around her this time.

Instead, her eyes glowed red. Her hair suddenly looked electrified. And she smiled. Then with a sultry walk she left the cabin without so much as a goodbye.

I cried. Deep heavy sobs. Kendi and I were never supposed to be apart. We were two sides of the same coins. Ever since we met, I'd been fascinated and in awe of her. I just wanted to see life through her eyes. How could the world tear apart a love so deep? It's a stabbing pain knowing someone you would die for resents you. All the love I thought I was showing her was received as arrogance. What could I have done differently? What could I have said to make my sister know I loved her like I loved myself? Honestly, I don't know if I could have done anything differently and that hurts the most. What could I have given her that was greater than my love? Maybe my understanding? Is the fact that I never truly understood her pain what separated us? I understand it now, having experienced real horror for myself. But back then, I couldn't have fathomed. I didn't know. And it's too late now. I laid my head down on the table and drifted into the sad abyss of my mind.

"Get up, girl!" The door swung open letting in the harsh light of morning. Emma walked in. Her face was serious.

"It's work to be done, girl, ain't no time for tears. Have you been by to see bout Rosalie?"

I looked up at her, eyes red and tired. I didn't respond. The hard look in her eyes got a little softer. She walked over and sat at the table with me. She was surprisingly swift for an old woman. I sat up straight, still silently crying, but ready to take in whatever verbal lashing I sensed coming from the tough old woman.

"I come from a long line of women whose mantra was 'get over that shit.' Growing up, whenever I would say something was difficult or uncomfortable, my mother would say to me 'cry for a little bit and then get over the shit.' It may seem like a harsh notion to grow up under, or a harsh way of raising children- specifically women, but it's necessary. Because as a woman, if you don't know how to pick up and get over that shit, you will surely die of grief.

Life is hard, and it's ten times harder if you'se a woman. Men will try to tell you that life is harder for them than it is for you. A man will tell you that the white man lays his burden on the black man's door. But what he won't tell you is that that same man will go home and lay that same burden on his woman folk. And his woman ain't got nobody to help her but God himself. So ima tell you like this- get over that shit."

I looked at her blankly and she smiled. She was missing her front two teeth, but she was so beautiful. She reached out and grabbed my hand, and then her smile was gone.

"Okay now, Lesedi, I ain't fixin' to fuss at you all day we's got work to do. Get yourself together and gone over and check on Rosalie. I gots to get back to the kitchen. You gone be alright?"

"Yes, ma'am. Thank you."

"Alright now," she said as she made her exit. I sat there for a moment. Then I wiped my tears and started my day.

When I knocked on the door to Rosalie's cabin, a strong voice called "come in." Rosalie was sitting up in her bed doing some needle work with a few pieces of fabrics.

"Feeling better I see," I said with a smile. She looked at me and tried to suppress a smile.

"I guess I owe it to you for reminding me I have something to live for. I'm living to see freedom. I ain't gone always be a slave. Ima be free or die tryin," she said it with seriousness and pride. I beamed looking at this little feisty woman filled with power.

"Well, miss Rosalie, I'm living for the same thing. Maybe we'll get there together," I winked at her and smiled as I made my exit. She studied me as if trying to decipher the words unspoken between the lines. One final look back on my way out the door confirmed to miss

Rosalie all her questions that were unasked. And I knew I gained another soldier in my army.

When I exited Rosalie's cabin, all hell was breaking loose outside. People were running in every which way. Swatting and covering their faces. There was a loud buzzing in the air mixed with the yells and chaos of the voices retreating. Using my own power, I cleared an aerial pathway. Wind whirled around me like a protective cyclone. Now tapped into my senses fully, I could make out the sound. It was the buzzing of bees. I looked up and was taken aback. Swarms and swarms of bees littered the air. On the ground in the distance was the body of the son of the master there encased with angry swarming bees. People were running and yelling and swatting as bees flew in every direction. And off in the distance, resting against a tree and playing with her long pointy nails was Kendi. Her hair was an electrified mess with bees nested all in it. She smiled evilly.

The sounds of hooves approaching caused me to snap my head back. It was Charles. He rode straight to me with eyes wide. "What is happening?" he demanded. I was speechless, not knowing how to respond. He got off the horse and walked towards the wind circling around me. "What did you do?" he screamed. Before I could respond, my hand was being pulled and an arm around my waist was leading me away. Ukize.

"Kize! Stop, just give me a minute," I yelled over the buzzing.

"We have to go now, Lesedi!" At that moment, a swarm of bees was flying towards me all in a straight line as if coming in for the attack. I could see Kendi with her long lean fingers and sharp nails spread wide apart as if directing them like a puppet. My eyes turned cold. Now I was mad. This bitch. After all I'd given her. Has the nerve to attack me and my man.

"Kize, go to the cabin and check on Dillon. I need to take care of this," I said calmly. I felt the white gleam in my eyes, so I know he saw it. He looked as if he wanted to argue but did not, he instead gave me a nod and ran off. The bees were swarming all around me now, but unable to get close because of the swirling wind I was encased behind. Did she really believe her power was stronger than mine? With one sharp move I summoned a loud deafening crack of lighting that hit a branch of the tree Kendi was standing under. She screamed and jumped back, breaking her hold and concentration over the bees. I walked towards her fuming. She had no idea what she had done; how she has compromised all we'd fought to keep hidden.

She was on the ground and scrambling as lightning continued to crack all around, snapping branches and darkening the sky. It was then that I noticed Charles was still watching from atop his horse. Of course, he never had to flee the bees, because Kendi would never send them on him. But he stared at me now as if seeing me for the first time. The wind blew through my long curly hair, and I relished its power, feeling it strengthen me. The grounds were empty now as most of the people retreated. The master's son also lay on the ground nearby half-dead, but still breathing. How much had he seen? Kendi watched me eye the blistered and bleeding man on the ground. She said in a shrill voice, "Don't feel bad for him. His fate is sealed. He tried to corner me and take me as his pet. He thought I was a weak woman he could have his way with. But I vowed when I left that slave ship, I'd kill myself and that man before I'd ever have my body taken again. And then you gave me this," She gestured towards the bees still buzzing around her and smiled wickedly.

"Don't you realize what you've done? Kendi, you've exposed us." I screamed.

She laughed.

"You're the queen of lighting! I don't understand why you just don't burn this whole place to the ground and be done with it," Her voice got dark now, and her expression changed. "What is it? You're too pure to kill? Or too weak?" Her voice was mocking me. With a swish of her long nails, the half-dead man on the ground was again swarmed by the bees. He shook violently and blood dripped from his mouth before his eyes stilled. I gasped in horror and Kendi laughed. Charles yelled from his horse to me "we must go now! We can't stay here!" he galloped towards me and extended a hand. I pulled myself up on the back of the dark brown stallion.

"CHARLES!" Kendi yelled in agony from under the tree as she ran towards us. I snapped another large branch that barely missed her head as I mounted the horse.

"Charles, where are you going? Wait!" she yelled frantically.

"Lesedi is right. You ruined everything we've worked to keep hidden. I hope it was worth it." He turned and slapped the reins of his stallion. Kendi yelled his name again before sending a swarm of bees headed our way. I turned my body and extended my arms out in front of me, my left arm atop my right and my wrists touching blasted a vortex of wind in her direction, sending her tumbling into the dirt. The thunder cracked again in the dark sky and rain began to fall. Charles was racing on his horse as fast as he could through the rain. We ran right past the slave quarters and headed towards the barn. On the way, I saw a gator walking the dirt path slowly, as if enjoying the rain on his scaley back. I looked into the gator's eyes, and he winked at me. I smiled inside and said to myself "Hi, Baba."

The weather had turned to a full-on thunderstorm by the time we reached the barn. We needed not to be seen and the weather was the only thing that was keeping everyone indoors. Inside the barn, Kofi and Kwame seemed to have been waiting on Charles. We entered hastily. Charles wasted no time telling Kofi and Kwame that we had been compromised and would therefore need to start the rebellion now. How Kendi killed the master's son, and how the slaves around her cried out and called her a witch. And in all sense of the word, she was. Giving her magic may have been a mistake, but even though the situation is what it is, I was still not sure if I'd say it was a mistake so soon. Only time would tell. I learned Sky Mother has a way of doing things that seldom make sense to me until time has revealed the reason.

Charles then said to the Akan warriors "send word to whoever you can. We leave at nightfall. There's no time to waste." He then looked at me and said "Kendi is a problem you created. So, you need to be the one to fix it." I nodded my agreement, not knowing how I felt about being given directions from Charles, but deep down, I knew he was right.

We left the barns and Charles said "I need to go spread the word. I assume you can make it back through the rain?" I nodded yes and he rode off in a flash. I ran through the mud and rain to Dillon and Ukize's cabin. I entered a wet muddy mess. Dillon and Ukize looked on with wide eyes as they eased me down into a chair and handed me a cup filled with a warm broth.

"Pot liquor," Dillon said. "It's full of vitamins. It's good for you. Emma makes greens for the house and brings us the broth they were cooked in. That's where all the healthy parts that were boiled out of the collards go."

"Wow, Dillon, how did you learn that?" I asked, shivering but still intrigued.

"Emma taught me. She says its why she still moves around so good at her old age."

Ukize rested his large hand on Dillon's shoulder and gave him an approving nod. Dillon eased away making room for Ukize to come closer. He knelt in front of me and began removing my muddy boots and garments. Nearby was a cauldron of hot water and a towel. He gently wiped the mud away from my face. I sat there frozen watching him move with so much love and care.

"What is the plan, my queen?" he said in a harsh whispered voice.

I looked into his eyes, and in the same hushed tone replied, "it's time to go." He stopped mid-movement and his eyes met mine.

"When?" he asked.

"Nightfall," I replied. He nodded and continued with the rag, dipping it back into the hot water and wringing out its contents. Just then, Emma stumbled in with a wet and dirty Rasaq behind her. "Baba!" I cried as I ran into his arms.

"We ain't got time for all this. We got to go now! The girl has gone crazy!" Emma said sharply.

"Emma, what girl? What are you talking about?"

"Kendi! She came into the big house with her bees and killed them all! Bodies everywhere. It ain't safe here no more. Master had dinner planned with Master Lindon Fields who owns the fields plantation about an hour's walk from here. Me and the girls have been preparing for it all day. Soon someone's gonna come looking for the master. And when they do, they'll hold us all responsible."

We all looked at each other in horror.

"Then let us pray," I said, eyeing them all one by one. They all nodded their agreement. We came together and held hands in a circle around the table.

"Sky Mother and all the ancestors who were made in her image. I first ask you humbly for your forgiveness. I ask that you remove the feeling of hate from my being and fill me with the strength of your goodness. Lead us down the path that you carved for us. Give us the power to save each other. Lead us to freedom. Let no weapon against us prosper. Create an impenetrable fence around us from our enemies. And when the time comes, provide me the strength to brandish my rod and my staff, for their powers comfort me. Create a space for us to start anew. And bless all those who come to aid in the fight. Thank you. Ase."

"Ase" and "Amen" were heard all around the cabin. Emma then said, "Let me go prepare and let Rosalie know to do the same and meet you back here."

"Where are we going?" Dillon asked meekly. I knelt down to meet his eyes.

"To freedom, baby. You're done being a slave. It's time for you to be who Sky Mother intended you to be: A king." I smiled sweetly at him, and he smiled back. "Now let us prepare."

I would make one more batch of the tonic. I was down to my last few petals, but I had to make sure we were as strong as we could be together. Especially now that I knew Rosalie and Emma would be traveling with us.

"Where are we going?" Dillon asked, his voice full of innocence.

Ukize and I said in unison "the Swamp."

# CHAPTER 20 *UKIZE*

The plantation was eerily silent. Whispers of the witch and her bees were circulating and stirring up fear; a true recipe for disaster. Time now was of the essence. Every move counted, and therefore must be calculated. In my panther form, I roamed the grounds, hidden in the long grassy stocks of sugarcane and stalking in bushes, searching for any sign of impending danger.

Just as Emma had predicted, a white man accompanied by two slaves showed up that evening. They pulled up to the unkept mansion expecting to find the master. They instead were greeted by the view of blistered and bloody bodies lying in the vestibule. But upon a second look, the master twitched. It seems he wasn't dead after all. The white man instructed his slaves to carry the man to his wagon. They exchanged a quick look before complying silently. In a dry croaked voice, the master said "she's a witch. The nigger woman with the wild hair is a witch."

They carried him to the wagon and rode off. He had said Kendi was a witch and used what I now know is a disgusting slur against my people. Suddenly, I knew the witch hunt was on. But who would they come for? My Lesedi has wild hair too, although not as electrified as Kendi's. But she was in the cotton fields this afternoon during the storm. And Lesedi has been healing slaves. Everyone with yellow fever had made a complete recovery. And after all that happened with Franny, what would everybody say? Would Kendi expose all she knew of Lesedi and betray her? I ran as fast as I could back to the cabin and told Lesedi all I had seen. She and Dillon were in the middle of packing for the trip. This was the beginning of the end; the final journey; the final descent. We packed healing herbs, medicines, vegetables, fruit, seeds, and smoked meat. I made sure to grab a few knives and blades I secretly forged in the blacksmith shop. One sharp enough to slice bone, the other with jagged ridges for tearing flesh.

The plantation gave the feeling of being abandoned for the rest of the evening. Most slaves had locked themselves up in their cabin, afraid of the African witch that had executed her revenge in a terribly savage way. The only sound to be heard was an owl hooting out in the distance. At first, I ignored it, but when it continued, I looked out the window. Seeing the big golden eyes, I ran to the back of the cabin. Lesedi looked over my shoulder unblinking, eyes and ears as alert as a predator.

"It's John," she said with wide eyes. I recognized the name being one of those on the list of people she told me were a part of her newfound tribe. He flew in the window and transformed.

"Sorry to barge in on you like this, but I was on the road and saw your master on the back on Lindon Fields' wagon," he said.

After making quick introductions, Lesedi gave John a quick run-down of all that had transpired. The look of shame on her face when admitting she had put power in the wrong hands made me angry; angry that she had been put in this position; angry of Kendi's betrayal; angry that the once bright and cheery girl I used to know was fading right in front of my eyes, and there was nothing I could do to stop it from happening. Life had a bleakness now, and its strong hold had a tight grip on our reality.

"I ran into Charles on the road a few minutes later. He's down in the old mill meeting with a few generals," John said. It didn't take long for us to decide to head that way. After instructing Dillon to stay hidden, and to run in his panther form if anyone came for him, we set out on a quick descent to the old mill.

Upon walking in, Lesedi and I discovered Charles huddled on the ground around a small fire, drawing tactics in the dirt with a stick and whispering to the two Akan warriors. Kwame, Kofi and I had bonded early on this plantation, being the only three men here who spoke the languages of the motherland. It was something sacred and also hidden. The Akans and I exchanged terse nods.

"Welcome, queen," Charles said in an unwelcoming voice. "I hope you are ready for battle. The time is upon us."

"And what exactly is your plan?" Lesedi responded with her eyes narrowed.

"I sent a message with the two slaves who accompanied Lindon Fields today. A message that all the generals should prepare their troops and prepare to move before sunrise. We have to move now, while they are vulnerable, and before they have time to call for reinforcements."

"Charles. This is crazy! What are you going to do? Burn down every plantation in the county? We need to run now! Not stay and fight them all. There's no way we can win. Don't you see that? We need to take a different approach," she pleaded.

"Stupid girl! This is the price to be free! Did you forget you were kidnapped, beaten, raped, and chained! Do you think they will respect you enough to let you be free without bloodshed?! Grow up!"

Before he could say another word, the crunch of my fist connecting with his face rang out. Charles spit out a little bit of blood and held his face. He looked up at me with a shocked expression. I looked down at him snarling.

"Where I come from, we show respect to our women. And this is our queen. You will show her your respect, or I will teach you how."

Charles looked up to Kwame and Kofi as if he was waiting for them to intervene, but they did not. Their people shared values similar to ours, and there was solidarity between us because we understood and honored that. The Akans stood unmoving, only observing. Charles' face was red as chilis.

I then turned to Lesedi. Her eyes were full of emotions I couldn't read. I said to her firmly, but with care "Freedom is not free, my queen. It comes at a price. We have been taught to seek peace. But we have also been taught to protect what is sacred, at any costs. So, we will fight, and we will run, and we will win."

She looked at me and nodded, each head nod stronger and filled with the fire I knew burned her from the inside out. She turned to Charles and said,"I will fight alongside you. I will instruct my warriors to do the same. But you must promise me you'll come back for Kendi."

"No. She›s too much of a liability."

"You will come for her! That is not negotiable!" Lesedi snapped, her voice trembling. John, speaking for the first time, said to Charles. "It's best that way. She knows too much. If they capture her, who knows what she'll let slip?"

"And she won't leave with me. At least not quietly. She'll only do it for you. Promise me Charles, you won't leave her when the time comes!" Lesedi pleads.

Charles looked to the two Akans who only nodded. He then said "fine. But if she gets in my way or does anything to jeopardize the mission, I can't promise to keep my word."

"Fine. We will head into the swamps tonight to warn my warriors and join forces with the maroons." She looked at me as she said it as if looking for me to confirm. I nodded my head as she spoke.

"We will begin our march into the city tomorrow before sunrise. I will meet you on the Rosseau plantation. For that'll be our last stop on our way to taking over the city. We will start north at the Lindon Fields plantation and burn everything in our path from there to Congo square. Be alert. Have your people ready. There's no going back now."

After leaving the old mill. I headed back to ready Dillon and Rasaq for our departure. Lesedi stopped to let Rosalie know what was happening. She wanted to give her the option of staying or leaving.

I wasn't surprised when Rosalie was in our cabin with a knapsack hanging sideways off her body, and eagerness dripping from her very being.

We let Emma know as well. With wide eyes, she looked at Lesedi and asked "My Esther. Is she running wit ya?"

Lesedi looked back with disbelief.

"You're the mama Esther said he wouldn't leave without?" Lesedi said, putting puzzle pieces together in her head.

"I knew you seemed so familiar. It's Esther that I see in you."

Emma wiped a tear away and spoke.

"I's going with you. Been a slave all my life. I ain't got too many more years left. But what I do got, ima use trying to be free."

"This trip won't be easy," Lesedi said.

"But I have something prepared that will help you on the journey. The two women drank the tonic. Purple glows emanated all over the room. When the task was done, Emma's dark brown skin took on the likeness of bark. Her hair had changed to tinged shades of brown and green. It was falling from her head like vines. She was the walking embodiment of a weeping willow tree. Rosalie seemed to be attracting all the precious metals in the vicinity straight to her hands. She was literally magnetic.

At dusk, we huddled together in Rosalie's cabin. Not a lot of people knew she was healed of the yellow fever and would deliberately avoid her. That was the main reason for abandoning Dillon and I's cabin and coming here. Emma brought us up to speed on what some of the other slaves around the plantation had been whispering. Emma heard all and knew all.

"Not all the enslaved people here will support an insurrection, you should know that. Prepare to have some push back, and maybe even some betrayal. Knowing the trouble it could bring and not wanting to see their only home and community destroyed would push some folks to defend their masters." Emma's voice held concern and also understanding. Lesedi voiced her awareness of this issue, vowing to not make the same mistake that she made with Kendi.

It was a cloudy moonless night. The sky was pitch black. Normally we'd use the stars to direct our path, using their location in the sky to tell what direction we needed to go. But tonight, we only caught glimpses. We didn't know the land or the terrain and had no clue where we were going.

"Stop. I have an idea." Lesedi's eyes glowed and suddenly the clouds had dissipated. The night sky was glowing vigorously. Not long after, we heard the sounds of dogs off in the distance.

"If we have clear visibility, that means whoever is out here with us does too," Rasaq said in a whisper.

"I can see clearly," Dillon said lowly. "I can guide us."

I could see clearly too. It was a gift from the panther. But seeing clearly would be no help if we didn't know where we were going.

Emma said, "I think I can help." She closed her eyes and stood rooted. She slowly transformed into a beautiful weeping willow. Her hair was transformed into long rippling vines delicately waving its lush leaves. And then a long line of green moss grew down her side. The weathered face of Emma appeared in the bark.

"Moss faces north." she said airily.

We all breathed a sigh of relief and began in the opposite direction of the moss.

"Dillon, you travel at the front of the pack with Rasaq. Emma and Rosalie will take the middle. The queen and I will take up protection from the rear," I instructed.

And we began our long harrowing journey into swamps. We traveled quickly and quietly, using our newly restored powers to enhance our senses.

The journey was long and exhausting, but our adrenaline powered us through the night. The nocturnal creatures of the land were out as well. Snakes, owls, bats and racoons. Even a few foxes and coyotes. I watched and listened as Rasaq communicated with them all. His power was immense. Emma's moss started us in the right direction, but it was the help of the animals that led us to our destination. Rasaq was hushed but still so lively. Elated to be back in his element. The father and ferocious gator had shifted into a snake we encountered. Next a bat, flying overhead to ensure our continued journey went as smooth as possible. Rasaq was in his element. The impending possibility of being free, and an opportunity to reconnect with the Earth and its creatures revitalized him in ways seen and unseen.

Lesedi walked quietly with her hand in mine. She too noticed Rasaq's affinity to the dark forest. She smiled slightly when he flew as a bat and moved clouds when we needed light or covering. But her gaze and her focus were on our surroundings and Dillon. She was uneasy with him being in front even though he was under the leadership of Rasaq. When I asked her what was on her mind, she simply responded, "battle is no place for a child."

As much as it hurt me to say it, I knew I owed my queen the truth. I turned to her and said "he will likely battle for the duration of his life. It's best he gets acquainted with it now," she stopped and looked at me before saying, "and why is that, how do you know that when we escape, we won't find destiny and live out the rest of our days in peace." She was upset.

I held her hand in mine and said, "because Sky Mother has given us too much. We will always have something we have to protect."

As we advanced deeper into the night, the smell of the swamp began to waft over us. We were close. Rasaq was a gator again, going ahead to test the murky waters and lead us in the right direction. The only sound in the night was the rustling of leaves and the chirping of crickets. The air seemed cooler but thicker.

Trees of mostly mossy cypresses and willows were growing right out the water. The silence was thick. And then slowly, bodies materialized out of the darkness. Emerging from the waters and trees were black bodies with painted white faces. A quick look up in the trees showed more bodies with bows and arrows aimed directly at us. A thin tall brown skin woman with locked hair and a gun strapped across her chest smiled and spoke.

"I've been expecting you."

The woman then smiled and said, "maroons, you may disengage."

# CHAPTER 21 *FRANNY*

The swamp was still today; too still. No ripples of water in the murky depths; No sway of willows in the wind; No call of the birds. It was a sign that something was coming.

"You feel that?" Octave's voice was steady, like a general preparing.

"Yes. I can feel it in the air. The nothingness is very telling."

"But what is it?"

I rubbed the cowrie shell around my neck between my index and thumb; a nervous habit. I took a deep breath and looked to the earth. A long slender branch was laying at my feet ever so conveniently as if it were waiting for me to need it. And I did. I picked it up and swirled it in the water of the swamps. Small ringlets began to rotate, and purple and green glimmers began to peak out from the center.

"What do you see?"

"An army moving. But this army... it's of ...animals? I see a spider,

235

a black dog, a gator, a panther, wait no, two panthers."

"Nahh, Franny look again. You been in that moonshine today girl?"

"Shut up, Octave, I'm trying to concentrate. The animals aren't really animals, their slaves. But they have magic. And the bearer is with them. She controls the wind. And she has women with her, all mothers of nature."

"So, what do we do ladybug?"

"We wait. Soon enough the path will be set. Ready the maroons."

Madame DuPont had warned me about this; even went so far as to tell the name of the chosen daughter the Gods sent from the motherland. Ever since then, I›ve been anxious. Anxiety is familiar to me. "Nerves been bad since a yout" as my mama would say. I miss her. Miss the island of Jamaica. Miss the mountains I lived in with mommy and the rest of the maroons. Many years I've been trying to get back home. To avenge that one fateful day that changed my life forever. I thought it would never come. Then one day, Madame said there was a message in the cards for me; a message from my queen mommy, who in my time away had gone on to be with the ancestors. Mommy said there is still a home in the mountains for me.

Later that evening, I was lighting candles when I saw the eyes of the gator approaching the shores. I stopped and grabbed my spear, thinking of what I could make for the colony with its meat and hide, when the stubby legs grotesquely reconfigured to a strong dark man with matted hair and a thick beard. Sprinkles of gray hair were all throughout his face and hair. I stilled with horror before remembering the army of animals in my earlier vision.

"I am sorry if I alarmed you, but my instincts tell me you have been expecting me." The voice was kind, but also fierce.

"I was expecting... well I don't know what exactly, but I didn't think I'd be visited by an African gator man. But I'm happy to see you nonetheless." He grinned and it was atrocious. Even though he was in human form, his grin was still very much gator. But his eyes were friendly, and I could tell by his energy that he was an ally.

The citronella oil candles and torches I had been lighting worked effectively to repel mosquitoes and insects. The oil came from the stems and leaves of a perennial grass called Cymbopogon nardus. It was one of the ways we adjusted to living in a decomposing body of water.

"What is your name, friend?" I asked the friendly gator man.

"My name is Rasaq. I'm here on behalf of my daughter, who is chief of Elegua and on her way here now as we speak."

"I can't wait to meet her. Madame DuPont speaks very highly of her."

"Her heart is pure." The look in the doting father's eyes said many things. There were so many emotions circling in this man. His energy was so overpowering it was hard for me as a reader of energy to be around him. He was truly powerful. And I had no doubt his beloved daughter was just as powerful as him.

"And you came here to meet me first and make sure it was safe for her to arrive," I stated, already knowing it needed not be a question.

"Yes," He replied simply.

"You know, this maroon colony began with voodoo. We were being chased by slave catchers. We tell the children how we were able to shapeshift into a hawk to find a safe place. Then the crocodiles allowed us to cross on their backs to the dry land centered in the swamp. We ran here for cover and nature protected us. You and your family are always safe here as long as you continue to honor Mother Nature."

"Who's this, ladybug?" Octave's deep voice was smooth. His wide stacked body made a menacing shadow in the candlelight.

"Ladybug?" Rasaq asked quizzically.

238

"It's Franny. Octave just calls me ladybug. And before you ask, only he can call me that."

"Why is a warrior named Ladybug, I'm curious?"

"Because, she's good luck. My granny would always say if a ladybug landed on you don't swat it away, it's good luck. And it just so happens she landed on me just as an insect would, and she's been my good luck ever since. But that's a story for another day. How many are you traveling with?"

"Six of us all together: Two men, three women, one man child." "Go and tell them they are safe. We will prepare a place for them." Octave and Rasaq shook hands. A mutual respect flowing from them both, and then the gator man was off.

A while later the six runaways arrived dirty and exhausted. Octave hugged the older woman tightly. She patted his face as a grandmother would her child. We led two of the women and the child to a small shaky cabin back amongst the trees. It wasn't fancy, but it was a shelter. Lesedi, Rasaq and Ukize refused to rest, instead opting to stay awake and talk strategy.

"I need to find a way to get a message to the Rousseau plantation. The last time I crossed the swamp, I was seen. I'm uneasy about going about it the same way I did before."

"I can help with that," I replied coolly. "There's a maroon here that grew up on that plantation and visited it frequently to see her grandfather until he died recently. She's accustomed to getting in and out unseen." I whistled the sound of a raven. From the darkness, Mary Jane emerged.

"Is it time?" she asked. An array of weapons was strapped to her body with animal hides.

"Not quite but it is near. The chief here has a message to deliver." All eyes turned to Lesedi. She was in deep thought. After a moment of consideration, she said,

"Rachell is whom I need, but she works in the house, and it may be difficult to get to her. Masozi will be the most accessible. In the slave quarters, his hut is in front of the garden. There's a blueberry bush behind it. Find him."

When she said that, the two men that accompanied her eyed her curiously. She must have noticed it too, because she said to them both "Sky Mother chose him." That seemed to have appeased them, because they gave no argument. She turned back to Mary Jane and said, "Tell Masozi to meet me in a dream. He will know what it means."

Mary Jane nodded her agreement. A look of discipline lined her face. She covered herself with a cloak and took off running. Lesedi and her family gawked at Mary Jane as she ran at lightning speed. They obviously were caught off guard by her swiftness.

Lesedi said to the men that accompanied her, "you two should rest. I'm going to make an altar and pray, and then I'll rest too."

"I think I will do the same. See you in the morning." Rasaq kissed his daughter and went off in search of a sacred space.

"Let me show you where you can sleep," Octave said to Ukize. Ukize's eyes fell on Lesedi.

"I'm ok, Kize, go rest. I'll be there in a minute." He grabbed her hand and kissed it lightly before following Octave into another shabby hut off in the darkness.

"May I borrow a candle please?" Lesedi asked.

"I can do you one even better." I led her to the small hut off the back of the shack Octave and I lived in. Inside were many candles and a few sacred trinkets I'd kept dear over the years. They were all surrounding my mother's ruby encrusted gold ring.

"I will leave you now, please stay as long as you need to." She pulled me in for a hug. As I exited, she began pulling her own sacred trinkets out of her bag.

"Say hello to Queen Mommy for me," I said before closing the door and heading into the darkness.

# CHAPTER 22 *MASOZI*

I was lying awake in my cabin. Sleep had evaded me lately and tonight was no different. Things around here had gotten progressively worse since Lesedi was sent to the Jackson plantation. Ben was acting like a madman. He had joined forces with Wayne, and the two of them began their reign of terror on the slaves here. Master Andre was so happy to see his wayward son take interest in the family business, that he'd given him free reign among the slaves. A week ago, George had been beaten bloody for passing out in the sugar house. He'd been overworked and under rested. The heat of the sugar house mixed with his fatigue almost killed him. Then they forbad the women from tending to him. When Julie took him some stew Ben tried to have her whipped. It took for Rachell to step in and ask Zoya to come to Julie's defense, which she did reluctantly. Zoya warned Rachel about interfering in business, and from then on refused to do any bidding on behalf of the slaves. Rachell was told to separate herself from the field hands. That it was a slap in the face to her mother and the master that Rachell had chosen to befriend the field workers, rather than spend her days being a pampered slave to the big house. It infuriated Rachell. Since then, the tension between Rachell and Ben could be seen slowly building. Today all assumptions were made clear, when Ben who usually works in the fields was seen riding horseback monitoring the field hands, and Rachell was outside with us chopping cane with her machete.

She stood by my side in the fields, and a friendship instantly forged. I assume it was because biologically she is my sister, even though I am sure she is unaware. Today in the fields, she looked so blank. I tried to comfort her by saying "you should only be in the fields for a little while. I'm sure your mama will have you back inside in no time."

"No," she said angrily. "That's not it. I don't give a rat's ass about whether I slave inside or outside. It's all the same. What hurts is that all these years, I thought mama and I had a special relationship. I thought she loved me. It was always clear to me that Ben and I worked while mama didn't, but I never questioned it. All the kids here worked. But now, I'm starting to see clearly for the first time that mama's loyalty has never been to me, or Ben. It's always been to the master. He provides a soft life that she enjoys, and she won't risk it. Not even for me."

"Or for me," I added quietly. Her eyes darted to mine. It was then I decided to tell her the story that constantly replayed in my head. As I recalled the details of that day Zoya entered my cabin Rachell's eyes filled with tears. She looked at me fully for the first time. She shook her head in disbelief and disgust.

"You look like her, only your eyes are different. I can't believe I did not see it for myself," she said through soft tears.

"You should know, that although Zoya has not now and probably will not ever be a mother to me, I will be a brother to you. You have my loyalty. Honestly, you are the only real family I have."

Rachell smiled. "And you have mine, brother."

Brother. She called me brother. Something so simple, yet so profound. It was providing me with a comfort I had never known. My baby sister. A deep love filled my chest. It's for her I would now live. I've made a mess of my life thus far, but slavery gave me something I didn't have back home: a family. And my mind was resolved that I would die for our freedom. It was this very thought keeping me awake now. And that's when I heard it. Outside of my window, there was a swish of wind. Inaudible to the regular ear, but my senses have since turned feline, and I heard all.

I got up from bed and pulled on my trousers but remained shirtless. I sat quietly and waited. A few seconds later, my window was being opened, and a small figure in a hooded cloak climbed through.

"May I help you," I said calmly from the chair I was perched in. She jumped a few feet and grabbed her chest.

"Jesus, you scared me."

"I scared you, and you're sneaking into my cabin."

"This is not your cabin. This was my grandfather's home. You are merely a visitor." I eyed the small, cloaked woman curiously.

"Kojo was your grandfather?"

"How do you know Kojo?"

"He was my friend."

She looked at me before responding.

"I am only here to deliver a message to you from Lesedi. She has asked for you to meet her in a dream. She said you would understand."

"I do."

"Great. Then my work is done. God be with you, Masozi."

"Wait, what is your name?"

"My name is Mary Jane." The woman removed her cloak, and she was stunning. She had cropped hair with tight coiled curls. Her skin was shades of dark brown and red. Her features were defined. She had a thin nose, thin lips, and straight white teeth. Her slim waist widened to accentuate her slim curves. Before I could think, my feet were moving and I was approaching her. She pulled a gun from some place unseen and pointed it straight at me.

"Don't move." Her face was serious. I smiled. I was entranced by her. She had dried mud caked on her scowling face and she was still stunning.

I took a step towards her, smiling coolly. When I heard the cold click of her gun I stopped in my steps.

"I don't want a fight, warrior queen. I just want to know more about you. Kojo never mentioned he had a granddaughter nearby."

"If you take another step, I will send you to the ancestors," she said unsurely. I chuckled.

"They will send me right back. They're having fun with me right now. It's been miserable you know, but meeting you is a step in the right direction." She eyed me curiously. She looked as if she was moving to speak several times but never quite got the words out.

"I won't hold you. But I hope we meet again, Mary Jane."

"God's speed, Masozi."

She wrapped herself back in her cloak with lightning speed and was gone before I could utter another word.

My thoughts went back to the words of Lesedi. "Meet me in a dream," she had said. This time when I laid down, I drifted away quickly.

Inside my dream, I was moving through a dark abyss towards an amber glow. I was in some sort of tunnel. The walls looked to be sand or clay and configured like a maze. I walked down numerous hallways until finally walking into an empty brown room. There were plants in the corners, and torches in the walls. In front of me was a long table. Lesedi was sitting crossed legged on the floor as if in meditation. She opened her eyes and looked around pleased.

She turned to me and said, "good, you made it. Please come sit."

I followed her command. I sat on the floor facing her. She extended her hands to me and motioned for me to lay my hands on top of hers. I did as she wished. She closed her eyes, and suddenly my mind was invaded with visions. They were her memories. She was on another plantation and so much was happening. A vision of a gator man, a panther and its cub, and then there were bees. When I opened my eyes,

I understood clearly what she had shown me.

"Battle is upon us, Masozi, and it is you that must lead." Her voice was stern. At that moment, voices sounded behind me. I turned swiftly to find Kojo sitting at the long wooden table along with Lyabo, and two other women I'd never seen before.

"Mama. Mama Oni" Lesedi cried. Tears spilled rapidly from her eyes. The old woman spoke.

"Hello my beautiful girl" Lyabo smiled.

"Daughter, I am so proud of you. You found your baba and your tribe. You have done well," the old woman crooned.

"Thank you, Mama. I am so sorry you were left alone; that I could not be with you when you crossed over."

"Don't worry yourself with death, child. You can't control it and it doesn't concern you. Sky Mother was kind to me. She did not let me suffer alone. She brought me here in my sleep to the realm of the ancestors where I could watch over you and my son from above."

Lyabo spoke again. "This is Eva. Who Franny referred to as queen mommy."

"Her mother?" Lesedi breathed.

"Yes, indeed child," the big dark skin woman said in a Caribbean accent.

"It is an honor," Lesedi replied and bowed her head. I bowed my head too, following her example, but couldn't help to peak back at the radiated souls before me.

Just then, a woman's body appeared out of nowhere at Lesedi's side. She was also seated in a meditation position with her eyes closed just as Lesedi had been when I arrived. Her eyes slowly opened and ballooned twice their size.

"I knew you'd be here," the woman was smiling and blinking back tears.

"I am always here," Eva replied.

Lesedi smiled in the woman's direction and said, "glad you made it Fran."

I looked at Kojo, who was beaming at me.

"Masozi of Oya. The ancestors are pleased. However, the work is not done. Man›s greatest battles are the ones he fights within himself. You did the unthinkable when you betrayed your people. But then you achieved a most honorable task. You made the change within. You have learned if you are building a house and a nail breaks, you do not stop building. You change the nail. You have proven yourself worthy despite how you began. Sky mother has placed within you the heart of a Lion. It is time for you to see yourself for who you really are, and who Sky Mother made you to be now and for always."

Kojo's words were so moving, I was speechless. I bowed my head and closed my eyes in gratitude.

"Charles has started a rebellion. He has completely ignored the fact that Robert Jackson is not in fact dead. Ukize saw him carried away by Lindon Fields' slaves. I am sure in no time, an army will be sent to dismantle Charles and all who march with him," Lesedi spoke out loud, looking directly at Lyabo.

"And that means us," Franny added. "We maroons will stand alongside Charles and Lesedi to aid in this fight for freedom."

The ancestors were all smiling, a complete contrast to our serious faces.

"We know what it is you are facing. We have only come to unite you and bless your journey. The three of you have been chosen to lay the foundation for future generations. You will each lead a group to freedom. One of you will travel south with a group of Black pirates who call themselves the Marauders. They are an elite group of maroons who raid illegal slave ships and transport stolen Africans to freedom. One of you will travel west out of the American territory. You will be protected under the Spanish crown as you establish the first free black town in western territory. The last of you will travel North accompanied by the Natives. Your settlement on the croaked Cuyahoga River will be a hub for future slaves escaping enslavement." Mama Oni added.

"Masozi, your task now is to prepare your tribe, so that when Lesedi and Franny arrive with Charles destiny can commence."

I nodded my agreement firmly. I wanted there to be no mistake that I take my responsibilities seriously. What an honor it was to be chosen. After all, I'd done, and all I'd been though, I was still chosen to be great. To be better than great. And this time, I wouldn't let them down.

I jolted awake to the navy-blue sky of the early morning. I quickly dressed and left the cabin. I said a quick thank you to those above and headed out the door. I had work to do.

# CHAPTER 23 *CHARLES*

I was born on Lindon Field's plantation. From as far back as I can remember, I was forced to be a man. Forced to deal with issues of man, and to handle business like a man. Some of us were never granted the luxury of just getting to be a boy. My mama couldn't protect me. She couldn't protect herself. The master was obsessed with her and took her whenever he wanted. My Pa was a big, strong man. He was dark skinned and burley. He was a carpenter and woodworker. He loved my mama, but he hated her too; hated her for something she couldn't control. And he hated me even more. The constant reminder that Pa could never protect mama, even with all his brute and strength. The master took his frustration out on Pa, because he hated that mama loved him. But he wouldn't sell Pa. Maybe because Pa was too valuable a slave, maybe because he wanted to make him suffer. Either way, Pa took that anger out on me.

I never had a place. Always too yella to be black and too black to be white. Unwanted, everywhere and by everybody, except my mama. But then mama died, poisoned by the wife of Lindon Fields was the rumor, and I knew it was true. After that, Master sold me and Pa. Couldn't bear to look at us now that mama was gone. Word is he never took up his wife's bed again. The tension and hate between them inside that beautiful mansion is so thick you could cut it with a blade.

On Robert Jackson's plantation, I kept my head down. I didn't talk to nobody. Emma never made me talk, she just fed me. She looked after me. And as I got older, she stayed close to me.

I was seven or eight years old when I began running errands for the master. He and his wife took a liking to me because I was resourceful, strong, and most importantly, obedient. Master's wife would poke holes in biscuits and pour molasses in the middle for me sometimes on Sundays. When the master's wife and third son died during childbirth, the master moved me into the cellar to work within the house. At first, I was just to do his bidding, but then my favor from the master was in exchange for secrets. He wanted to know the whispers in the slave quarters and all the things the master couldn't see. What better way than through a child? After a while, the slaves here isolated me. I once again found myself a man with no place. The only place that was ever mine was with my mama, and maybe with Mandy too.

Once I was big and strong enough to man a stallion, I began running errands off the plantation for master. I was familiar with the Fields plantation, so that was a frequent stop for me. The first time I stepped back on that plantation after the master sold me, I was a man. A real man this time, not just a boy pretending to be one. Lindon Fields looked at me silently for many minutes. I thought I saw something in his eyes, but it quickly vanished. It was then when I met her. Working on the plantation I was born on.

Her name is Amanda. The day I met her she was doing laundry outside in an enormous hot vat filled with boiling water and lye, her loose dark curls. sticking to the sweat on her face. Her skin was like mine. Half-black. Half-white. I wondered if her mama whispered her origin to her like mine did to me. I recall the day so clearly, my mama sat me down to tell me why my Pa hated me. Why my Pa wouldn't look at me. Mother whispered the story to me of her own rape. It planted in me a seed of rage and resentment towards the white planters. I kept this rage a secret, and instead became the inside man. I wondered if her mama had said the same to her. If she held pain deep inside like I did.

After that day I couldn't get her out of my mind. So, one day on a Sunday I decided to ask my master for a pass to go visit her. He granted my request, and to my surprise, Lindon did as well. From then on, every Sunday I'd take my pass and go see Mandy. Many days were spent just talking to her. I never had somebody I could talk to before. I told her about my mama. I never told a soul about my mama. Only Mandy.

It was because of this same pass I was able to plan this parish-wide rebellion in secret. It gave me access to many slaves in many different places. It allowed me to establish a grapevine of communication. The minute I saw the bloody bodies under Kendi's hand, I knew it wouldn't be long until it all came crashing down. All I could think about was Mandy. I had to get her and my unborn baby to safety. This was all for them after all. This was my one chance to have the family I never had. To belong somewhere. And if I had a son, I'd make sure he'd get to be a boy, and not have to grow up to be a man so soon, like his Pa. And now they were asking me to bring Kendi along too. I couldn't let her know about Mandy. It was too risky. Kendi's mind is too unstable.

It was what made her such a great warrior. Where my Mandy was meek and proper, Kendi was wild and unapologetic. She was passionate and unyielding. Her fire ignited me. But she is not a wife. She does not obey, does not hold her tongue. She does not heal like my Mandy, only burn.

I suppose that is why I found myself caught between the two women. Healing with Mandy the parts of me I kept concealed and burning with Kendi, the other parts of me I also kept concealed. The battle inside finding solace in each of these women.

The general on the Fields plantation was a man named Elijah. I sent the signal with the slaves who accompanied Lindon to the plantation earlier to get Mandy to the swamps. Where she could be protected until I could return. Elijah could get her there. He was well connected but kept all his secrets to himself. Nobody knew how he did it or who he did it with. Everybody just knew if Elijah said it could get done, it would be done.

Now that I knew Mandy would be hidden. My focus drifted back to Kendi. Despite how furious I am with her for compromising the plan, I must admit now the way she commanded today set me on fire. Lesedi had said where she comes from, women lead. Such an unconventional concept. But maybe Kendi could be useful. Her new magic was impressive. I'd go back for her, bed her, and then lead her into battle.

That night in the darkness, I went to her cabin, but she wasn't there. It was inside the now empty big house I found her. In the master's suite. Lying in a four-poster bed among white cotton sheets and quilts. Candles were lit all around, and Kendi was simply seductive. We spoke no words. I walked towards her while removing my shirt and grabbed her by her neck. She only smiled. I kissed her fiercely and took her right there in the master's bed.

Afterwards, she looked up at me and smiled.

"I knew you'd be back," she said in a smoky voice.

"You and I have work to do," I replied flatly.

"I know that too," she countered before slipping into sleep. I did not sleep. I laid there wide-awake anticipating what the next few hours would bring.

While Kendi slept I raided the house. Adding any ammunition, guns, first aid and weapons I could find inside an old carpet bag stored in the closet. It was almost time. Passing the large bathroom off the master suite, I decided I'd take the time to wash. Not remembering the last time, I had been able to, and realizing I may not be able to again for a while. I heated the water and carried it up the stairs to pour into the clawfoot tub. The warm water settled over me. One last minute of peace before all war broke loose. Then I dressed and went to Kwame's cabin. He was awake and waiting on my alert. He'd man the plantation now. I mounted my stallion and hit the dirt road in the velvet black of night. Behind me were ten men on horseback, ten others stayed behind under Kwame and Kofi's leadership. Under the veil of night, we set out for the Fields plantation.

Kwame and Kofi were the key to this rebellion. Although they preferred to play the background, they were the brains of the operation. I am their selected general. It was them who figured out slaves in the Parish outnumbered their white counterparts fifty to one. Their home- The Kongo was torn apart by civil wars. Prisoners of war often ended up as slaves, through betrayal or capture. This is how hundreds of veterans trained in military practice and combat happened to be on this side of the Mississippi, Kwame and Kofi being a perfect example. Still burning with the passion of war, they were willing to use force to obtain freedom. It was under their leadership and their warrior knowledge that this rebellion took shape. Their close ties to Miss Dupont were the most crucial part, the madame herself a descendant of Akan warriors, the ancestors reunited them here for this very task.

Under their direction, spies and lookouts were positioned everywhere from inside the French quarter to perched in the trees outside plantations just as they did in Africa.

It was early just before dawn. The black of night still reigning over the land. The rain that had resumed meant time off work in the fields because of the flooded soil. The muddy ground made it difficult to move around. When I reached the hidden part of the forest that would lead us to the Lindon's plantation, I held up a hand to signal to the horsemen behind me to halt. My eyes searched the night. A faint airy whistle lightly called out. I followed the sound. The old and round uncle Phil was waiting by a tree stump. Uncle Phil touched his straw hat and led the way through the stacks of out-houses, past the sawmill, to the sugar mill. Weaponry collected from the Lindon plantation was all stored here. Elijah entered from the shadows. His short and wide stature made him appear to be shaped like a perfect box. A stocky build, with skin the color of roasted coffee and wavy black curls. His affinity for the mother Mary, and his romantic way of speaking were tell-tale signs of his African and Spanish ancestry. How he came to be a slave was a story he refused to tell.

"Is she safe?" I asked.

"Si. She is safe."

I nodded my thanks, and we began the business of rebellion.

We entered through the back door of the big house with knives, machetes, axes, and guns. Some of us stormed the second-floor landing while others lined the elegant walls in the shadows of the halls.

When we stormed into the room Lindon Fields, he woke startled. His eyes were fixed on the black faces and machetes surrounding them. Fields, my biological father, recognized me at once. Fury filled his small eyes. He lunged out of bed and tried to make a run for it, his wife who was in her suite down the hall, had also heard the commotion and came running into the belly of the beast. They never made it down the stairs. Both of their bodies were apprehended and promptly diced like fruit. We emerged from the house victorious. A fire was set, and thus the drums began to sound. Men off in the distance patted their hands on the hollow instruments, sending an ominous ambiance over all that heard it.

Slaves began to emerge at the sound of the drumming with curiosity and confusion painted on their faces. I was back atop my stallion with the ten men I rode with behind me. Elijah also was horseback. 20 men were behind him. I called out to the onlooking crowd of slaves.

"It's time for you to determine once and for all where your loyalty lies. Join us and march to your freedom or stay here and wait for your death!"

"We risk death following you!" a voice yelled out from the crowd. A few murmurs of agreement followed.

"Then you will remain a slave. Those of you who are not afraid, join us! Come fight for what is rightfully yours!

Bodies began to waver and soon, the crowd was moving. Some in the direction of Elijah, others back to their cabins. They had made their choice. We had to march on. We set fire to the mill and the house, then headed back to the Andrews plantation, soldiers, weapons, and drums in tow.

We started with around 40 or so enslaved men when we left Lindon's plantations in flames. We collected more men along the way as we stopped at the Andrews, and Jackson plantation to collect the rest of the soldiers and set fire to the place I had called home all these many years. Kendi smiled radiantly as the flames danced. She joined our ranks, riding on her own stallion beside me. Her hair was circled high into a wild nest, closely resembling a coarse beehive. Her buzzing companions followed her faithfully. Small groups of enslaved people joined from seemingly out of nowhere as we marched. We carried mostly pikes, hoes, and axes, and a few firearms, as we marched to the war drums. The rhythms being beat out weren't just rhythmic beats, they were formations. Taught to us by Kofi and Kwame, we knew every rhythm had a special meaning.

The news of the rebellion seemed to have spread fast, as a few homes along the way that belonged to white families looked to have been deserted. Off in the distance, you could see the black and orange fumes of fires. The sounds of drums were still loud in the air. Traveling with so many men, women, and children ended up being more difficult than I originally envisioned. The muddy conditions made traveling at this capacity nearly impossible, but still we muddled through.

During the day-long fifteen-mile trek, we burned everything in our path. Several sugarhouses, and crops popped and cracked as the flames engulfed them. Ruin lay behind us as smoke filled the air. Devastation taking over the once fertile lands.

We were a motley crew of warriors. Kendi was alongside me, her long nails the color of honey, and bees buzzing behind her forming their own ranks. Together we marched to our final destination before claiming Congo Square, The Rousseaux plantation.

# CHAPTER 24 *LESEDI*

I couldn't get up. I knew what I had to do, and I was prepared to do it, but for some reason, I just couldn't move. I felt weighed down. The physical heaviness of weariness was pressing me against my chest and pinning me to the floor I slept on. Ukize was calling my name, but I couldn't respond. I laid there feeling stuck.

All this fighting, all the trying, all this running. Why? Why such a life?

"Lesedi..."

I didn't answer. Now free from the invisible hold on my being, I shifted on my side, turning my back to him.

"Listen. I know you're tired. You don't have to tell me what you saw last night, I can look at you and know whatever it was is a heavy load. But you've got to get up. If you don't do this, it won't get done. I know it seems an impossible task, but the way I see it, you have nothing to fear. You were made for this; designed for this. Every single thing you have done in your life, even something as insignificant as the stories you asked to be told to you over and over as a child, all helped shape you for this. Look at what you've done. You have survived. Against all odds. You should have been dead many times, yet you are here. Moving in the shadows, unseen and unscathed doing God's work. Get up my queen. Right now.

I turned to him, feeling overwhelmed and anxious.

"I'm scared," I said in a shaky voice. It was all I could get out. The tears wouldn't come today. I'd cried enough. But Ukize didn't say anything. He gently put his hands under my arms and pulled me up to face him. And then he pulled me into a hug. A big bearlike embrace that covered me fully. Just a hug. A simple act of love. And I started to feel that load suppressing my chest lighten. I was breathing a little easier.

"I miss my mama. She was so good at being chief. She always knew what was best and what was right. And she used to hug me, just like this."

"Your mama is with you now. She is in you, Lesedi. You are more like her than you know. The daughter of the poised queen and the gentle gator."

I laughed. For the first time in many moons, I laughed genuinely. I felt Ukize's chest rise and fall as he let out a chuckle.

"You know what my mama's power was?"

"No, what was it?"

"She had the power to heal what ailed people in their heart and mind; to remove trauma from their very soul and replace it with love and gratefulness. She was a tough woman, serious and strong. But she carried the gift of clarity with her everywhere she went and shared it with everybody."

He laced his fingers between mine. "That explains where you get it from. That is what you are doing here now: Honoring your mother's legacy and your father's too."

I looked up into his melancholy eyes. "How do you deal with it, Kize? I know you miss your mama and baba and your siblings. Yet you're always so strong; strong for me, strong for Dillon, strong for everybody."

He breathed a heavy sigh, and in his baritone voice said "I cry, Lesedi. At night while I lie awake. It is very painful for me every day. I do not sleep anymore; I only think. I don't know what became of them that horrible day, my family. But I pray that they are safe, and I pray that

LESEDI AND THE PURPLE LOTUS

they are well. And I honor my roots. I am an Eleguan man. I know that. I won't allow any stranger in this place to tell me differently. Slave or nigger, I am neither; I am a warrior, raised by men of honor. So, every day I repeat that to myself, and it gives me strength. I find my power in remembering."

I nodded. He was right, and I had never been as grateful for him as I was now at this very moment. By speaking his own truth, he freed me from my bondage.

"And you are the strongest of them all. The greatest warrior I have ever known. And the only man I will always love."

I rested my head on his shoulder as he rested his on top of mine, our hands still interlaced.

"I am ready, my love. Let us go." I turned to face him, and he gave my hand a gentle squeeze, and we began to prepare for what was to come.

When Ukize and I exited the shack, Dillon was outside playing with Rosalie. She had her hands over the earth, summoning arrowheads that had been lost beneath the soil. Dillon watched with amazement as he inspected the triangular pieces thoroughly. He smiled and ran into

268

Ukize's arms as we approached him. It was only then I noticed all the people.

At least 50 or more men, women and children were all around; most notably, the group of warriors with painted white faces who were readying weapons. Baba appeared from the center of the group with a wide grin. It wasn't a happy grin; It was almost scary; It looked hungry. When he caught my eyes on him, his expression changed. He approached me and delicately pulled me into a hug. He looked down into my eyes and then closed his. As if to take in as much of me as he could.

"I'm going to be ok, Baba. Don't worry."

"I know," he whispered. "I know."

Franny's appearance was also menacing. Weapons were strapped all over her toned and muscular slim physique. Octave was at her side. Strapped to him were two guns and a band of ammunition. Warriors stood ready for battle all around.

"For you, my queen," Ukize opened his huge hand to expose a small and deadly blade.

"When I made this, I didn't know it at the time, but I was making it for you. Keep it near."

I stood on my toes and kissed his cheek. He gave me one last look then left my side.

Ukize, and Baba were headed to join the men who were giving instructions to the young boys. Dillon listened intently alongside the others. It made me uneasy, but I knew Ukize would not have it any other way. After all, he was around the same age when he entered the bush.

The children were given bows and arrows and told to sit in the trees. They'd be spies, and lookouts, silent assassins in the trees. But hopefully it wouldn't come to that. The children took their roles seriously. They all walked off to claim their tree. Rosalie would stay with the children and protect the swamp with a group of maroons.

"Dillon," I called lightly. He turned and walked towards me with a gleam in his eye. The innocence of childhood.

"I want you to be careful today, do you hear me? Rely on your power. Be the strong, brave panther I know you are, and I'll be back to take you to our new home."

"Yes, ma'am," he said as he wrapped his little arms around my waist. I hugged him back and kissed his brow before releasing him.

"Do you hear that?" Octave was looking towards the sky and a hush came over the swamp.

"War Drums," Ukize answered.

The faint sound of a beating rhythm could be heard in the distance. We quickly gathered ourselves. Baba, Ukize, and I painted our faces white like the maroons. I braided my hair in two long plaits and wrapped them on top of my head in a tight bun. And then in the new morning sun, we exited the swamps.

I found myself again treading the dark waters of the swamp. But this time, we walked low through the water, keeping our bodies submerged so only our noses and eyes were seen. The drums were getting louder.

Coming down the road were Charles and his army. The smell of smoke hung overhead and blew through the breeze. Charles and his generals were mounted on horses. Each leader was commanding a group of rebel slaves, some on horseback, others on foot. One of the leaders, a stout dark man with wavy hair, was swinging his saber in the air. Behind all the mounted generals were no less than 300 escaped slaves, all armed with machetes, garden tools, axes, and ice picks. Only half had guns. Sounds of horses' hooves, paired with the drums, were heard all around. And then a most ghastly sight gave way.

Approaching from the southern end of the road were three companies of volunteer militia under the command of the badly injured Robert Jackson. Along with them were 300 armed soldiers from the U.S.

Military. And we all knew they were there to stop the escaping slaves.

"Gentlemen, attack!" Jackson was heard yelling clearly through the disarray. Clicks and bombs rang out deafening the atmosphere. Smoke clouds filled the air and men screamed. Canons boomed. War cries and men counting in intervals overlapped with the sound of gunfire. We emerged from the swamp and scrambled to find safe positions. Out of the corner of my eye as I ran, I saw men charging and bodies falling. We were all separated now. I spotted Franny running alongside Mary Jane in my direction.

"We need to get people to safety! Clear out the slave quarters and get them to the swamp!" I yelled over the rumble of chaos. I took off running towards the cabins and Franny and Mary Jane followed.

Nanny was in the cabin with Tilly, Lilly, and Esther. In my time away, Esther's growing belly was more obvious. Nanny said she ordered Esther to bedrest. This pregnancy had been harder on her than the first. There were two other children there too. Scared, they cowered in the corner. Tilly was reassuring them everything was ok, while Nanny was over Esther who was in bed with Lilly.

Once we knew they were safe, Franny and I quickly went to work protecting the cabin. We burned sage all around. Before leaving, Franny threw salt over the threshold and circled the cabin. It was behind the cabin where we found Masozi and the whole crew. My heart was so happy to see them all. Now was not the time for pleasantries. I'd tell them all how much I loved and missed them once this was all over.

Masozi called to me. His tone and demeanor was like a soldier's. No, more than that, a general's. He was strong and confident as he spoke to the group.

"The Master and Zoya are still in the house. There are a few slaves with them inside. Ben has formed his own group of resistance under master Andre's orders to assist the militia in defending and preserving the farm. If we are going to get anybody off this plantation and to the swamps, we will have to first pass them, and then the militia. Charles seems to have them tied up so the quicker we can get out the better!"

"I will station wherever you need me. I can get slaves to the swamp. Nobody knows the lands in between as well as I do," Mary Jane responded.

"Then, it is settled. Mary Jane, you shall stay here behind the cabins. But you'll need a second."

She looked to Masozi. He met her gaze and responded "I am needed elsewhere. Jake, will you stay with Mary Jane and protect the cabins? It might be good to have a pack of dogs around just in case."

"Of course," Jake said firmly. Julie nodded her approval and Jake squeezed her hand. He knew just as we all did that Julie was strong enough to manage while Jake helped her.

And again, we all dispersed. But this time, we were using our powers as our shield.

Masozi was a gorgeous yellow-gold lion. His strong, compact body and powerful set of teeth and jaws were on full display. He took off running with a growl.

Rachell took off running behind him, fire gleaming in her eyes as they headed for the big house. I ran to the nearest cabin to see who was inside. I wanted to make sure all those who wanted to get off the plantation knew which way to go but, when I turned the knob to enter, I was met by the scowling face of a black man with a gun pointed at me.

He was dark and skinny. Almost gangly, with veiny hands and arms and a missing tooth.

"Looks like I'll be getting the reward today," he snarled. "Have a seat right there and don't move," he used his gun to gesture towards a table and chair in the corner.

I turned with a defeated look and headed in the direction of the chair. The man grinned, his face shiny from sweat or grime, or both. With one quick motion, I got low and spun my leg around in a swift kick, breaking the leg off the table. Before it hit the ground, I blasted a vortex of wind beneath the greasy man's feet, and he fell to the floor. I grabbed the table leg and twirled it like a staff. Today, it would be. It whistled in the wind as I twirled it. The man scrambled for the gun that he dropped when he fell. I spun my staff across my body and smacked it into his hand. He screamed in agony. He tried to roll to the other side, but I spun my staff again and drove into his side. He arched and squealed.

"Now. You're going to tell me what I want to know, or I will beat you bloody," I kicked the gun across the room and placed the staff into his neck.

"Why are you here?" The man didn't answer. I released my hold and twirled my staff, so it whistled once more.

"Okay, okay!" he screamed. "I was sent here to stop y'all from stealing the master's property and ruining the livelihood around these parts. Some of us have worked this land our whole lives. My daddy died working this land and is buried on this land. It ain't right for y'all to come burning things down and messing up the natural order of things. And it just so happens there's a reward for any slave that stops a rebel. And ima get me that reward."

I looked back at him confused.

"You do know we are here to fight for our freedom, right? Why not just choose to be free?"

He laughed. A cold unhappy laugh. "Be free and do what? Struggle? Suffer? Live in the swamps among the wretched insects and swamp monsters? Here, I have my own cabin, the same cabin my daddy had. I eats out the garden, and Master gives us pigs. Why would I leave all this behind to go into uncertainty? That don't even make no sense."

"And where is your mama?" I asked angrily.

He looked down. "Master sold her when I was a boy."

"So, what makes you think your position is safe here? Why do you defend the man that sold your mama? Your father died alone and as a slave! And you will do the same if you don't wake up!" I was furious and screaming now. "Tell me, what has he done?"

The man was now wearing a look of defeat.

"He emptied the quarters when he got a midnight telegram about the rebellion. Slaves are locked in and piled up on top of each other in the storm cellar until this is all over. The storm cellar is behind the house, and Master got Ben and Wayne perched outside protecting it. They've been told to shoot anyone who approaches."

I looked into the eyes of the man lying under my staff.

"Are you an enemy or a friend?" I asked.

"Neither." He replied.

I grabbed the staff and left the cabin. All I could think about was getting to that cellar. The man did not chase me as I went to leave. He didn't even get off the floor. One thought did seem to cut through my focus. If the master had the quarters cleared out, how was it that nanny and Esther had managed to occupy the cabin still with the children?

# CHAPTER 25 *MASOZI*

Lions are known to stalk their prey before attacking. Our sudden and surprising aggression causes prey to panic and disperse. But their speed and power are no match for the mighty lion's. I used their own panic to isolate them. Then attack. And as I ran through the tall grass, I eyed my target.

Combat was happening all around. The plantation had become a battlefield. Black and white bodies littered the ground, but the sounds ringing overheard told us it wasn't over yet.

Lesedi was running through the grass. Rasaq, who must have spotted her, ran her way at lightning speed.

I contorted back to my upright body. I motioned for Rachell to get low. We were hiding in the tall grass stalks of sweet sugarcane. Rasaq and Lesedi soon saw us and did the same.

"He has them locked in the cellar," Lesedi breathed.

"You two go. Rachell and I will cover you," I breathed back. There was no way to approach the house without being seen. Ben spotted Lesedi immediately and raised his rifle at her. Her eyes were glowing white, and she manipulated the wind with her hands to redirect the bullets. As she worked, she never stopped walking. Slowly she was getting closer and closer to where Ben stood guarding the cellar door. He shot at her repeatedly and her walk got slower as she carefully manipulated the flight of the ammunition. Rasaq's expression was downright terrifying. His African features had shifted back into the essence of a gator. He walked upright and strong, but his skin was a shade of greenish brown, and his teeth were replaced with sharp razor-like blades. His wide fingers transformed into long dark claws, and with one frog-like leap he was on top of Ben looking down into his horrified face. With his sharp claws, he ripped into the barrel of the gun before digging his claws into Ben's shoulders.

In his African accent, he leaned in and said, "Who are you?" Ben did not respond. Rasaq stood upright and laughed. He turned to the spectators and said loudly, "You see this? You see the sadness, eh? He turned back around and said to Ben directly "What are you afraid of?"

Ben was in complete and utter terror. Then in a deadly whisper Rasaq repeated "Do you know where I come from? I come from de jungle! WE come straight out de jungle and in de jungle, there is no refuge!"

He pointed around and there we all stood, unknowingly assembled all together and looking on at the escalating situation ready to react.

James' black skin had fluffed up into fur, as he stood on his hind legs as a ferocious growling bear. He pounded his paws on the ground and charged towards the house moving in big leaps. Rachell and I took off running behind him. Her hair was on fire and her eyes were red. Soldiers were headed in our direction to defend the big house. Overseer Wayne and Master Andre both exited the house carrying long shotguns and ammunition as they stood on the big house porch.

Lesedi was working to get the cellar open, but it wouldn't budge. The battle was leaving Charles and coming to us now.

As the soldiers fired their muskets, clouds of smoke rained down and covered everything. Guns roared and bullets hissed through the air. The ranks of militia and military and planter sympathizers formed themselves in a linear formation. Guns aimed and exploded as they carefully kept formation.

Luke's face was crawling on the massive body of an eight-legged arachnid. He leaned back on his haunches and raised his head and legs. Long curved fangs were exposed as he squirted a nasty acidic liquid into the line of soldiers. They screamed and grabbed their melting faces as they fell to the ground. The line behind them stepped over them and aimed in unison. And then, one by one, the line of soldier's bodies dropped. Their eyes turned black as gray smoke-like ghosts floated and dissipated. Lucy was there, her eyes completely black. She had released their souls, and now lifeless bodies lay in the balance.

Julie was seen now approaching the porch where the overseer and master watched horrified as Lucy collected and released the dark energy. Rachell and I walked behind her. We had to get into the house.

Julie removed a flower from her hair, a purple African violet. She blew on it, and purple dust surrounded the master and Wayne. Their expressions went from militant to lovelorn. She was using plant pheromones to lull her prey. Julie's expression then went from sweet to deadly. She turned to the soldiers firing in our direction and let out a loud grunt as she clapped her hands together. The earth between them cracked in half, and they fell down into a massive pit. The keys on Wayne's hip floated through the air on a breeze and landed right in Lesedi's hand. Sable then became visible.

Shots rang out again as another group of militia and their loyal slaves came around the back of the house. This time, Rasaq fell face first into the ground. Lesedi let out a mangled scream. Thunder and lightning clapped in the sky, making a thunderous boom. She dropped and flipped Rasaq's body, but his eyes were unmoving. Ben, who was now free of Rasaq's hold, would have undoubtedly died if it wasn't for Rasaq's body being the barrier. I ran into the group in my lion form slashing through flesh. I heard a growl nearby and realized Ukize was beside me as a panther, the two of us in divine feline power overpowering the bodies. I felt the sting of something ripping through my flesh and fell. I quickly tried to get back up, but my left arm was severely bleeding.

"Don't move," I heard the voice say. It was Rachell's. She was a walking flame. She walked towards the line of fire, and for the first time, they broke rank as they scrambled to escape her blaze. She ignited everyone she touched.

"Don't y'all even worry. I'll clear all this out," she said as she moved. John came galloping up, dressed in leather and holding two guns. His head and large yellow eyes seemed to move on a swivel like an owl's. His horse powered through, almost as if knowing where to go and not needing John's direction. His eyes were big and ominous as his head turned to the back of his body. He let out two shots, and Andre and

Wayne fell to the ground. John didn't stop to look back as he righted himself on his horse and kept riding.

The banging and shooting finally died down. A sign that each side had retreated, even if only briefly, to collect their injured. Lesedi, whose face was contorted in a way I'd never seen, was using the keys to open the cellar. Ben jumped behind her and wrapped his arm around her neck as if to restrain her. She reached into her waistband and pulled out a tiny blade. It was barely visible. She sliced back one time, and Ben fell to the ground holding his gut. Lesedi ignored him and opened the cellar. Brown terrified bodies spilled out. Lesedi instructed those who wished to leave to go to the quarters and collect whatever they could. Rachell assisted me into the house, as Ukize ran to Lesedi.

Rachell and I finally moved to enter the house, stepping over the bodies on the porch as we crossed the threshold. Rachell led as I followed her up the steps. Soft sobs were echoing from a room at the end of the hall. Zoya sat on the edge of the bed with her head in her hands, slowly shaking her head in disbelief. When her eyes met ours, they were glaring.

"We've come to take you with us mama." Rachell spoke faintly." It's not safe here anymore."

Zoya scowled. "You made it not safe here. You and that demon woman. I saw her from the window. And she's turned you into one of them. I'm not leaving with you; hell will freeze over first. You ruined everything. All of this to do what? Be a vagabond slave hiding for the rest of your life?" Contempt was dripping from every word.

"We did it to be free, mama. Ain›t you tired of being a slave?"

"I wasn't a slave!" Zoya screamed frantically before breaking down into sobs. "But I will be now, all thanks to you," she said sarcastically.

"What about us, mama? What about your children? Don't we get to have you for once? I had no one. Baba was a drunk and you were gone," my voice cracked as the last word escaped; emotion releasing that I thought I had forever buried.

In a lazy response, she replied "I don't know how to be a mama, or a slave. I don't know how to do anything but what I've been doing. Now leave me to grieve in peace."

Tears fell from Rachell's eyes and sizzled as they landed on her hot skin. I held her hand and led her as I closed the distance between us and Zoya. Silently, I kissed our mother's head and walked away, not looking back. Rachell mimicked the motion as her grip remained firm on my hand. As we exited, she whispered "I love you mama. Now and forever."

# CHAPTER 26 *LESEDI*

A gain, I heard Ukize's voice around me, but it was muffled. I hung my head and cried. I watched my tears fall from my eyes to my Baba's handsome face. He looked now as I always remembered him, smiling and singing in the morning with the birds. I couldn't move, for although I knew he was no longer earthside, I felt his presence with me then as hoovered over his body. Ukize bent down and lifted my chin, so my eyes met his.

"The men and I will carry him. We must go." Ukize's voice was shaky. It took all his strength to keep his composure. I looked into his sad glossy eyes and put a hand on his face. Tears fell and dropped into the palm of my hand.

I closed my eyes, and a misty rain fell. Not the pounding pouring drops of a storm, but the refreshing mist of a spring morning. Clouds cascaded from the sky and smoothly slipped around Baba's body, encasing him in a glowing white casket of condensed vapors.

He floated in the center, and we walked along the sides of him.

Behind the slave quarters, the place that became a temporary home for me, were my friends; my new family, and so many enslaved people waiting to begin their new life. It was overwhelming. Somber and anxious energy washed over the atmosphere. Bodies were everywhere. I took a minute to take in what was around me. Masozi's arm was wrapped in a fabric drenched with blood. Charles' body lay nearby, lined up along the ground with more unfamiliar faces. Kendi was on Charles' side. They looked peaceful, as if they were only sleeping. The sight of them together filled me with so many conflicting emotions. Charles and I really never got along, but I felt the loss of him profoundly. He was stubborn and arrogant, but he had also been strong and persistent. There was no way we could have done this without him, despite our differences. We owe our freedom to him. And Kendi… my oldest friend, my sister. At his side, devoted even in death. I can't pretend to know what motivated Charles or Kendi. But their lives would not be in vain. I'd carry them with me always, honor them always, and tell their name to generations to come. They would be remembered for their sacrifice, not their trauma induced flaws.

Kize had a gash along his forehead and Luke was limping. But we were all here, and I took time to thank Sky Mother for that. I cleared my throat, and everyone looked at me.

"We must go now. I'm sure you all know how dangerous this journey may be. Anyone unwilling to cross the swamp and follow commands should go their own way now. If you choose to stay, you choose to fight." No one moved. There were about 40 slaves along with us and the maroons. Quietly, we followed Franny and Mary Jane as they led us through the dense forest into the swamp. We chose not to go over the road, as we didn't know how close the pro-slave military may be. Not long after we entered the woods, we heard the bark of dogs and the sounds of men. We stopped in our tracks. It was so quiet, it was as if no one was breathing. A pack of about 50 dogs was charging towards us. Some of the escaped slaves with us made a move to run, but Jake held out a hand. A smile curved his lips. When the dogs reached us, they all stopped and sat at attention. Jake whistled, and Belle came to the front. Belle howled long and loud and all the dogs turned about face. Jake's long physique was transformed into the muscular rottweiler with the gleaming black and brown fur as he went to Belle's side. Behind the dogs were more ranks of white soldiers holding artillery and weaponry. They were momentarily caught off guard once they realized the dogs were now snarling at them. They loaded and aimed their weapons towards the dogs who were enclosing in on them. When the first shot rang out, all hell broke loose once more as dogs charged, barked, and bit in every direction. It was only then I noticed the peculiar direction of the wind. It was circling itself and creating a cyclone. But I wasn't doing it. My power was focused on the cloud my Baba was still wrapped and levitated in. And that was when I saw Tilly. Her eyes were purple, and her long pigtails were blowing straight up as if standing on her head. She was protecting the dogs. Her cyclone blew over the soldiers as they scrambled in the leaves. Julie was standing beside her bringing branches down around the trees, encircling the militia in a prison made of braided vines and branches. Those purple pheromones from Julie's African violet reappeared and the men fell in a slumber. The branches on the wooden cage became thick with sharp thorns.

I turned and beamed at Tilly, shock and pride swelling inside. Jake and Julie were breathing hard with satisfied looks on their faces. It was beautiful to see how this family continued to fight for each other. It moved me and restored my fire.

"So, it was you Tilly; it was you that kept Esther, Nanny, and the children safe," I crooned.

She nodded.

"Esther is sick because of her baby. We couldn't let Master put her in the cellar with Lilly." She smiled up at Esther who was leaning on James. They both were looking at her with a look of pure love.

"And Nanny had been looking after little Paul and his sister Ruthie when Wayne and Ben came. I saw them out of the window. When they came close, I blew them away. They kept trying to come back, but every time they came, I made the wind sweep them up." Tilly made wave motions with her hands as she said it. A big smile spread across her round face.

I squatted down, opened my arms, and she ran into them. Julie was crying. Belle was at Jake's feet as he placed an arm around Julie's shoulders. Tilly's hug enveloped me. How could such a small child be so powerful? All that ached in me was soothed by the pure light emanating from her. With that, we continued on.

When we emerged from the woods, we were at the mouth of the swamp. Traveling with us were children, elders, and a pregnant woman. Many others were either injured or exhausted, or both. I knew crossing the swamp now would be a much harder feat than it had been before.

The sound of a horn barreled through the air. Waiting in tugboats on the bayou were more of the militia, waiting as if knowing where exactly we were headed.

"Damnit!" Octave spat.

"Don't worry, my love," Franny said coolly. "You see they can come no further than where they are right now. These swamp islands aren't easy to man against. We people of color are just made for it. When we first came, malaria ran rampant. White people would flee the swamps and all the surrounding areas in order to protect their immune systems. We Africans' immune systems are stronger because our bodies are made to be equipped for the native land, which is both lush and rugged. Anyway, when rumors first started getting around that there was an island for runaways down in the swamps, they tried to come for us. When the island was hunted by whites, they were immediately killed by Mami Wata, who is the soul of this swamp. It is she who protects us. They called us demons with dark magic powers, but it is not us who created the power. It is the ancestors whom we keep near doing the magic for us. Those whose blood is still within the ground."

Franny's words triggered knowing in me. I looked at Esther who met my gaze. "Wait here," I said to the group. I took Esther's hand and led her to the water. We walked side by side hand in hand as we approached the shore. The boat moved in our direction. We kneeled at the shore, our knees in the mud and our hands open and pressed on the cold and soft surface. And then the water shifted. Tall waves reached up in the air, sending the boats of militia on its side and then completely submerged. The waves formed into long locs surrounding a narrow face. and there she was: Mama. Esther was walking, but I stayed bowed. Every step she took, the water parted for her, clearing a long muddy path. Her long, wet dress clung to her high belly as she sparkled in the sun. Baba's cloud encased body floated down the path behind her into mama's large hands formed by the muddy water.

"Rest now, my love," her voice echoed as Baba's cloud disappeared into her body of water. "Come daughter, lead your people home."

I looked up. Mama nodded her encouragement. I stood and looked behind me at everyone watching me.

"Come. Let us go," I called to them. The group all began to walk the path that parted the water. Mama's gigantic water figure lingered in the air, as if shielding us from all that was unseen. This was so much like the processions we had back in Elegua when a soul crossed over from Earth side to the ancestor realm. Our traditions are so deeply embedded in the very fibers of our being, that they follow us, even unknowingly.

When we reached the maroon island, Mama's water body closed the path that opened to us and smoothed its waves. The sun glittered on the surface. Rosalie was waiting with the group of maroons she'd stayed behind with, a pile of guns in all sizes lay in a huge pile.

"We confiscated quite a few weapons while y'all were away," Rosalie chimed. Their stockpile was impressive. Everyone here would be back on the trail pretty soon. These weapons would be a godsend.

Dillon and the children were descending from the treetops and running into the arms of the adults they belonged to. Dillon ran straight to Kize, who held him tight. I wrapped my arms around them both. We all looked around and formed somewhat of a circle. We were dirty, bleeding, and a little broken inside. But we were alive, and more importantly, we were together. Franny walked towards the center of the circle. A few women followed her. They were each holding stone jugs shaped from clay.

"We pour libations for those who we have lost. When we do, we awaken the ancestors. In remembrance of their spirit, we vow to carry them with us forever," Franny poured a little of the fermented drink into the ground, and then took a sip for herself.

"For those we've lost," she said as the liquid entered the earth. Soon, stone jugs were being passed around as people took turns pouring a little out and taking a sip for themselves.

We spent the rest of the evening dressing wounds, cooking food, visiting with loved ones, and preparing for the next part of our journey. Esther was sitting with Lilly, James, both his parents who had escaped the Rousseau plantation, and Emma who was finally reunited with her daughter.

Dillon, Ukize, and I were sitting with Masozi, Mary Jane, Franny, and Octave. Franny and I had spent the last hour covering all who needed it with Imphepho. The plant is traditionally used as a wound dressing. Its antimicrobial properties worked effectively to kill bacteria and relieve pain. I'd be bringing this on our trek, along with a few other remedies. I wanted to have a few things ready for us to aid with any sickness that may occur on our journey out of slavery. As I walked around the island, I couldn't ignore the sound of buzzing in my ear. Eye level to me now was a plump black and yellow queen bee. I followed her. Deep in the trees, she led me to a hive that was dripping with honey. I retrieved a jar and collected as much as I could with the bee's permission. The birds were singing my Baba's song. Inside the jar was the honey I was given. I added lemons with a little ginger. It would be a valuable item to travel with. It would keep us in good health. It made me feel protected and loved to know Kendi and Baba had loved me now as I know they always have. This was their gift to me. Health and protection.

Sable, John, Lucy and Luke were talking to a group I recognized as workers from the Jackson plantation.

Julie was cooking around a pit along with a maroon woman. Jake, Tilly, and Nanny were sitting around the fire talking with a few people from the island and the plantation. The maroons had extensive networks of slaves on the plantations that provided them with food and warned them of impending raids. People like Monique DuPont, and John were their connection. It explained how here on the island in the middle of the swamp, we were able to prepare head hash, which is the head of a pig, chopped and cooked in broth with tomatoes, mustard, peppers, onions, and cinnamon over rice.

Some of the women were preparing maps that took form as quilts or braided hair designs. The intricate designs in the quilts and paths of the cornrowed braids were in all directions.

A pregnant woman sat on a stump with little Ruthie between her knees interweaving the pattern of the map in her coarse hair.

I watched her curiously, intrigued by her skill. The short stocky man whom I saw earlier with the saber was walking towards her with… Chief Running Bull? I excused myself and ran in his direction. We gave each other a hug before parting.

"You came back!" I exclaimed.

"I told you we would meet again when it was time." He turned to the pregnant woman and said, "I am so sorry for your loss, Mandy."

"As am I," the general added.

"Elijah, Running Bull, I don't know how I could ever repay you for what you did for me. My Charles may not have been able to live to see freedom, but our child will."

My jaw hit the floor. But I quickly composed myself, trying not to upset the woman.

Instead, I smiled at her and said, "you know, in my village, we have a saying. That if a child's parents should die before their time, then their lost years will be added unto the child's. If that is true then your baby and I will both live long lives. Tragic death will not be your child's portion." I smiled at her as the sadness crept in. She dropped a quick tear and smiled back.

Everyone on the maroon island seemed to be busying themselves. I took that time as the perfect moment to slip away. I entered Franny's shack where I had spent the previous night praying. I lit the candles and sat in meditation. Mama Oni's face lit up the darkness.

"Mama," I sang. She beamed. I dropped my head. "I lost Baba, just as I lost Mama. I am sorry I have failed you."

"You did not fail, child. You won! Let me ask you this, what is your definition of a hero?

297

I thought for a minute. "Someone who saves their people. Who does what needs to be done in order to live. Someone who chooses to do the right thing over the easy thing. That is what I view as a hero."

"Well, then you my dear are in fact a hero. More than that, because your power is superb. You are a superhero. A hero thrusts herself into her destiny. She knows the journey holds many perils, yet she carries on. When she is in her darkest and lowest place it seems, all hope is gone. But then through her values, her knowledge, and her power she emerges. God favors her, and she is victorious. Many are delivered because of her audaciousness. Now how would you describe that person? Would you still call that a failure? Or would they be triumphant?"

I thought about all I'd been through. The woman I was when I started this journey compared to who I was now. That day at the sacred center, Sky Mother tried to tell me this was my hero's journey. And Mama and Baba delivered me and continued the circle of life.

Mama Oni read my thoughts.

"Exactly! Look what you have done here. Successfully laying the path for our descendants to continue is not just a victory for your people, Lesedi; it's a victory for yourself. You all shall be remembered as super. You all have displayed super strength, super speed, super superhuman capabilities and a super ability to be resourceful.

We lost many but it is not the end. You've known a life filled with love and gratitude, growth, and power. Many who are generations removed from their homeland didn't know who they were. They had no idea they were gods living amongst mortals. They were shamed for having skin the same pigment as the earth for whom they were born from. The infinite earth is what rests in their veins. But they'd been oppressed in chains for so long that they forgot. But even though their mind forgot, the soul knew. It just needed a reminder. And the love you showed was that reminder. It is love that carries us through. Not just love for the family we were born of, but also the family we create."

"I understand now, Mama Oni. You mean our love of our culture, our love of our strength, and our love of each other is what powered us through. It's where we found the motivation to not give up. Knowing we must live, so those we love can live too has given us strength."

"That is correct my child. It is the core of what Sky Mother gave us. For we elders only desire to bequeath two things to our children. The first one is roots; the second one is wings."

# EPILOGUE

S pringtime- a concept. A time of new beginnings. Winter has always been hard for me. It has always seemed like the season of purge. It's only now that I recognize that that may not necessarily be a bad thing. Last year, around this time, was filled with so much uncertainty.

That next morning after battle, we all departed. It was an emotional day. In a short amount of time, we had been through so much together. As we made our departure, the decapitated heads on pikes reminded us of those we lost. Those who participated in the rebellion either found freedom or death. Those who were captured were brutally tortured, as to make an example for any other slave that may be considering following us. We had shaken the very core of the overstuffed planters. Among them were those of the mighty Kwame and Kofi. I thanked them all for their sacrifice, Kendi and Charles included. Their sacrifice would be repaid through the life we would live in their honor moving forward. A life free of bondage. They fought and died to be free of the chains that trapped our bodies and our minds; to flee the trauma and its tight hold. I pray their souls are free now. I pray that they now know glory.

Masozi, along with Chief Running Bull, headed North. Rachell, Mary Jane, Sable, Luke, and a group of the formerly enslaved from all three plantations went with them. A beautiful white quaker woman they called Aunt Kathy had arranged for them a way to travel safely through a network of anti-slavery sympathizers.

Franny and Octave took a group including Nanny, Esther, Lilly, James, his parents, Clyde and Maude, Emma, Mandy, and a host of maroons and ex-slaves. It was the best option for the women who were carrying, and the elders who could not brave the forces of nature. They would sail into Jamaica, guided by Mami Wata and Franny's queen mommy. That day of departure, they headed to the boatyard where they were met by a black pirate named Wesley.

As for me, I headed West. With me was Elijah leading our group with the help of his Spanish mother Rosalba, and a Black Seminole Indian named Diego. Also with me was Ukize, Dillon, Rosalie, John,

Lucy, the children Paul, and Ruthie along with their parents Anna and George, Jake, Julie, and Tilly. Thanks to John and Elijah, we were all able to procure our own horse. Rosalie, Jake, and George drove wagons to accommodate the children if needed. Rosalie's wagon was filled with guns, artillery, and ammunition, all confiscated from the pro-slavery sympathizers. Dillon, being the man child he was, rode horseback with us.

Elijah's wavy hair was a show of his mixed Spanish, Native, and African ancestry. He had been working with the Spanish all along. His mother, a wealthy Spanish woman, had become pregnant by a handsome African ranch hand. When the baby was born, he was kidnapped in the night and sold into slavery by her parents. But Elijah's mother had secretly found him, thanks to the help of Miss DuPont and Running Bull. It was she who whispered the path to freedom to Elijah. Dressed in our leather's chaps, and wide brim hats, we rode the red flat land past cacti and tumbleweeds as we headed west into the unknown territory to lay roots for what would become the first free black town.

After weeks of traveling through desert lands, we came across a lush valley. It was here we settled. My lotus had survived yet another journey, although missing a few pedals, it was stronger than ever now with my power being added to it. In the hard clay ground of the desert, I planted a lotus petal. Trees filled the valley, blooming lush purple flowers, and cacti baring the same purple leaves. The power of my lotus in the earth spread for miles and miles. It provided trees that fed and housed us. And life started anew for us, here in the lush valley in the middle of the desert.

Ukize and I were expecting our first baby to arrive on the eighth full moon of the summer solstice. On the night of the crescent moon, I had a dream. It was of Mama, Baba, Mama Oni and many other ancestors whose names I'd only heard in stories, but I recognized them right away. Mama Mazi and Mama Nakia, Auntie Abeena, and many others. They were passing a baby carefully down the line of ancestors. They were tender with the sleeping infant, handling them like a precious fragile treasure. I dreamt that dream every night until the full moon came. Every night meeting more and more ancestors as all carefully handled the baby.

My daughter was born in the darkness of night. A beautiful orange moon and many stars shone in the sky. Only the light of the fire we had burning illuminated the dark velvet atmosphere. And in the midst of the flames, she came screaming into the world. Her eyes were like a panther's, and her skin was just as dark. That night I dreamed again, but this time it was of a tall girl with panther-like eyes and dark obsidian skin. She was walking with a staff in one hand, and a bag strapped across her body. And illuminating her scalp was a purple glow.